THE SHELTON GANG: THEY PLAYED IN PEORIA!

THE SHELTON GANG: THEY PLAYED IN PEORIA!

. . . and they played WAR in "Bloody Williamson County"

Bill Adams

Library of Congress Number: 2004094347
ISBN : Hardcover 1-4134-6013-5
Softcover 1-4134-6012-7

The amazing story of the Shelton Gang and Family, including never before published information on their long career of controlling vice and crime in Southern and Central Illinois during and after Al Capone's Chicago reign!

Chicago was "Scarface Al's," but the rest of downstate was "Shelton Country" and they never let anyone forget it!

This book was printed in the United States of America.

To order additional copies of this book, contact:
Xlibris Corporation
1-888-795-4274
www.Xlibris.com
Orders@Xlibris.com

24927

CONTENTS

This book is dedicated to Flossie!

My wife of 60 years, and still my best friend and companion. But much more than that. She's my conscience, my sounding board and my most valued critic. Without her love, her support, and her unending patience, I could never have accomplished what I have over the years!

Preface

Three Shelton brothers, originally from Fairfield, Illinois, ruled a crime empire for over 20 years, on a scale never before experienced in central and southern Illinois plus St. Louis, Missouri and parts of Indiana and Kentucky.

For all intents and purposes, the Shelton "Gang" ended with the deaths of Carl Shelton in 1947 and Bernie Shelton in 1948. But recently information has surfaced that, for the first time, sheds light on many things that happened ***after*** the battles and "wars" waged in St. Louis and southern Illinois.

It mainly concerns the "wide open" Peoria days after Carl and Bernie were assassinated! They both met violent deaths in the way so many of their victims did . . . at the wrong end of a gun!

Later, the entire Shelton family either met violent deaths or, maybe worse, they lived with terrible violence that later nearly consumed the entire family, including their mother and a sister, after their father had died.

But no other "gang" was more successful, if you can call it that, and certainly none survived as long and through so many, now legendary, battles, as did the Sheltons.

One gangland battle turned into an actual war with armored vehicles on both sides and bombs being dropped from a plane.

The Shelton "Gang" at various times numbered 20 or 30. But the Shelton "Boys" meant only three of the five Shelton brothers who decided early on, that gambling and bootlegging was easier and more profitable than working for a living.

First there was Carl, the oldest "gang" brother, and the brains of the outfit. Next in age came "Big" Earl, a big farmer type who was shrewd, able and sometimes reckless. The youngest of the three was Bernie, the mean, surly one, especially when he was drinking.

If you saw Carl on the street and didn't know who he was, you'd take him for your average every day business man. He was soft-spoken, unpretentious and could be downright charming . . . but you'd better not cross him!

Earl was called "Big" Earl so as not to be confused with a nephew, "Little" Earl, who was also connected with the gang and was named for his uncle Earl but was the son of another Shelton brother, Dalta, who decided to farm instead of joining his notorious brothers.

Dalta also had another son, "Little" Carl, named for his notorious ringleader uncle, but he was not a part of the gang, although he did get into trouble with the law on his own.

The oldest of the five Shelton brothers was Roy, who had gotten into trouble with the law earlier and finally decided farming would be less troublesome but he also was later killed by a sniper while riding his farm tractor.

"Big" Earl was a huge, hulking man and during their rum-running days, transported the booze up from the south.

Bernie was a barroom brawler and rough-talker. He was the gang's muscle and, when someone didn't go along with Carl's wishes, Bernie would come in and break up the guy's joint . . . and probably the guy in the bargain.

In the 1920's and 30's Al Capone held reign in Chicago but downstate was Shelton territory, along with part of Kentucky and southern Indiana, and the gang left little doubt about that. Some tried to fight the Sheltons for control of it but, until Carl and Bernie were killed, no one succeeded for very long.

The three "boys" started their wayward ways in their teens and kept building their "empire" until the late 1940's when, first Carl and then Bernie, were ambushed and killed, just nine months apart. In 1947, Carl, riddled by bullets, was killed shortly after he had supposedly retired from the Peoria gambling scene and moved back to his Wayne County farm.

Then, nine months later, in 1948, Bernie was gunned down and killed outside the Parkway Inn on Farmington Road on Peoria's outskirts.

The only one left of the three "boys" was "Big" Earl, who also had a farm in Wayne County but someone was still after him there. He was wounded on two different occasions by snipers.

"Little" Earl was also shot at, along with another member of the gang, Ray Walker, when Carl met his death, and several more attempts were made on "Little" Earl after that.

These two "Earls" survived, but they did it by packing up their families and leaving the territory for parts unknown.

During the Shelton's quarter-century reign of terror in Illinois, one or more of the three "boys" were formally charged more times than can be counted.

They were convicted and served a small amount of time for a few of these crimes, but very, very few.

And as strange as it may seem, three of the brothers were assassinated; another was wounded twice; a nephew was wounded four times; and a sister and brother-in-law were also wounded.

Eventually the entire family was threatened and run out of the state . . . and not a single person was ever convicted for the crimes against the Sheltons.

None before . . . none during . . . and none after the Shelton Gang played in Peoria!

Chapter 1

The Shelton Family

The Shelton family began very unassumingly in southern Illinois, a part of the state known as Little Egypt.

Benjamin Marsh Shelton, the boys' father, was born on September 18, 1861 in Hopkins County, Kentucky, the son of Wilson Albert and Paulina Johnson Shelton. Paulina was Wilson's second wife. Before the turn of the last century, Ben came up to Wayne County, Illinois and married a local girl, Agnes Gaither, who was born on March 19, 1866.

The farmland around Merriam, Illinois, a small town about five miles east of Fairfield, was poor and sandy but these two hardy people began farming about 120 acres there, where most all of their ten children were born. Six boys; Roy, Carl Ray, Earl Robert, Bernie Bernard, Dalta, and Albert Lonzo, and four girls; Nora, Hazel, Lula and Blanche. Seven are known to have lived to adulthood.

The Shelton's oldest child, Nora, was born December 4, 1883 and died September 8, 1897, just before her 14th birthday. Nothing more is said about Albert and Blanche.

Of the five remaining boys, only one, Dalta, walked the straight and narrow path. Roy, the oldest boy, went to prison early on but, after a couple troublesome episodes with the law, stayed clean and lived the rest of his life as a farmer.

The Shelton children went to Sunday School in Merriam and it's said that, at the insistence of his God-fearing father, Carl taught Sunday school and played the organ at Beach Bluff church. The kids also attended a one-room grade school.

The Shelton's were tenant farmers and for a few years they farmed several hundred acres in what was known as the Elm River bottoms. They were doing pretty well, off and on, until about 1908, when a flood wiped out their entire crop. After that they ran a country store at Thomas Prairie for a couple of years before buying about 20 acres near Merriam.

Carl, Earl and Bernie didn't take to hard work, especially farm work, and they soon began stealing. One local man said they'd steal harnesses, horse blankets, buggy whips or anything they could get their hands on and everyone was afraid of them. Their father hardly ever spoke to his wayward sons after they became notorious but their mother would always insist that her boys could never do anything wrong.

On January 10, 1909, Carl married a girl named Lulu Woods of Fairfield, the daughter of Vess and Cordie Johnson Woods. They were married by Rev. Joseph Virgil Clark and it was witnessed by Fred Wilson and Iva Kuster. Lulu died a short time later. Then about 1912, Carl went to St. Louis and worked for awhile in several grocery stores. Later he got a job driving a taxi cab for the Columbia Cab Company there.

Earl also married a girl from Wayne County, by the name of Edith Gurley, on June 18, 1913. She came from a prominent family but she, too, died.

After that Earl started hanging around a pool hall on the Wayne County court house square and it was about this time he had his first run-in with the law.

His neighbor, Cloyd Wilson, had a horse and buggy and Earl often rode home from town with him. A local man stated that one Saturday evening Earl borrowed five dollars from Cloyd and then met him later that same night at about 11 p.m. to ride home. Wilson later told the following story:

"We starts out for home. Out by the cemetery bridge a fellow stepped out from the side and got hold of the horse and stopped him and told us to get out, it was a stickup. Earl got out right away and walked clear around the horse and stood by the fellow. I thought maybe it was a fake. But then I saw the gun."

The man took Wilson's money, a gold watch and a ring and let them go. The next day the sheriff arrested a man named Thomas Draper who matched the description of the robber. Wilson positively identified the man as the culprit. Earl maintained Draper wasn't the man, but another local man identified Draper's gun as the one he had earlier sold to Earl for five dollars. The grand jury indicted both Earl and Draper for robbery and conspiracy.

Wilson later said that Earl offered him $500 to drop the charge but he refused. He said Earl, or someone close to him, worked with the local politicians to get his case separated from Drapers.

Carl Shelton, who had been living in St. Louis, came back and began threatening Wilson. Then Carl sent two thugs from St. Louis to waylay him. He was warned, however, by Frank Crews, a cousin in St. Louis who said his wife had overheard the Sheltons plotting the plan. The Wayne County sheriff arrested Earl and Carl but later had to let them go due to a lack of evidence.

In St. Louis the Sheltons threatened Mrs. Crews and Crews reported it to the police. On June 12, 1915, Earl and Carl were charged with compounding a felony. Then Crews told the police that Carl and another man stole a car in St. Louis the previous year, and Carl was charged with grand larceny too.

Earl's case in Fairfield was continued until October, but on June 24 Draper was convicted.

In the meantime the Sheltons promised a vagrant a horse and wagon if he would lie to the police by saying that Crews had stolen a ring from him. The man agreed and on June 30, detectives went to question Crews. Thinking that they were Shelton's henchmen, Crews shot the finger off one of them and he, in turn, was shot through the lung. Crews was arrested but then released and freed of any suspicion because the vagrant confessed his part in the frame-up.

The Sheltons didn't forget Wilson's part in pushing his holdup charge against Earl. He and other witnesses were threatened all summer, so Wilson hired Fairfield's leading lawyer to work with the state's attorney.

It was said that one of the Sheltons had bought poison in St. Louis to kill Wilson's cattle. Then the Shelton's mother told the sheriff that Wilson's mother had attacked her with a butcher knife, but the case was thrown out of court.

Earl Shelton went to trial on October 20, 1915 and was convicted and sentenced to the Illinois state reformatory at Pontiac. He was 25 years old and served 18-1/2 months before he was paroled.

Chapter 2

Bootlegging and The Ku Klux Klan

Earl Shelton began serving time on October 20, 1915 and on November 11th, brother Carl pleaded guilty to petty larceny and was sentenced to a year in the workhouse.

Cloyd Wilson said this whole case had cost him over one thousand dollars and the loss of a summer's work. As it turned out, though, this became one of the most successful prosecutions ever brought against the Shelton boys.

After their jail terms Carl and Earl returned to St. Louis where their younger brother, Bernie, joined them. Bernie was later arrested when he was caught in a stolen car but was not prosecuted.

Little is known about what effect World War I had on the Shelton boys but it is believed that the only one to serve was Earl, who was said to have been in the Army for a short while and on his way to France when the war ended in November 1918.

After the war the Shelton boys moved to Carterville, a coal town in Williamson County, Illinois where they worked in the mines and Carl rose to the position of inspector. Their brother, Roy, also worked here and it's believed young Bernie may have also joined them for awhile. Later the company moved Carl to Herrin, where he lived for a brief time.

Roy Shelton, the oldest of the Shelton brothers was never connected with the Shelton "Gang" but he did run afoul of the law early on, which may have been the reason.

It was in Williamson County that he was convicted of burglary and robbery in April 1922 and he was sent to Menard state prison to serve a term of one to twenty years. He was paroled on good behavior after he had served part of his sentence but Roy made the mistake of violating his parole and was sent back to prison until 1931.

But in 1933 he was arrested again, this time for robbery and kidnapping. He was again convicted and since this was his second offense, not to mention violating a parole, this time the judge threw the book at him with a term of one to life, which was enough of illegal living for Roy. He was released in the 1940's and decided that it was better to work for a living and he returned to Wayne County and led the life of a farmer.

After Carterville Carl, Earl and Bernie started spending a lot of time in East St. Louis, an Illinois city just across the Mississippi River from St. Louis. It was a tough town notorious for corrupt politics, gambling, guns and illicit sex.

The three brothers pooled their resources and opened a saloon near 19th and Market streets, and they ran it as a legitimate place until Prohibition started in 1919. Then it became a speak-easy.

Bootlegging began and Earl started running illegal booze in from the south and the boys became distributors for the entire area.

Besides Earl's rum-running efforts from the south, a man named Charley Harris was driving liquor in for them from the east coast and Canada. Harris and Carl had grown up together back in Wayne County and became boyhood friends.

Charley was doing real well running illegal liquor until, on one of his trips to Canada, he made the mistake of purchasing a shipment to keep for himself. He had visions of becoming a free agent, but Charley had made a serious mistake. He thought he could make even more money if he paid for the booze with counterfeit money. He was arrested and Carl spent $1,600 in his defense. Harris was convicted anyway and was sentenced to ten years in Leavenworth prison.

Meanwhile the Shelton boys had made connections with East St. Louis politicians and also the gamblers, the kingpin of whom was a man named Charlie Birger. Their friend Art Newman was already a member of the Birger outfit, so the Sheltons threw in with their gang. It didn't take long, though, before the Shelton boys were running the operation.

With a stuttering roar, two Thompson machine guns disrupted the quiet of Ralph (Wide Open) Smith's East St. Louis beer joint one Saturday night in February 1931. When the smoke cleared Smith found himself with three bodies and a near nervous breakdown. He boarded the next train out of town.

The bodies, which were carried away and dumped into a Madison county ditch, were those of Joseph P. Carroll, tough ex-policeman and associate of St. Louis gang leader Tommy Hayes; Theodore Kaminski, a gang hanger-on and David Hoffman, East St. Louis pawnshop owner.

These killings were one incident of many used in a chart later prepared by investigators for Senator Estes Kefauvre's Crime Investigating Committee in the 1950s. The significance of the "Wide-Open" Smith murders might have escaped the crime probers had not the *St. Louis Post-Dispatch* come up with the information that explains them and set them up as key to the later extermination of Tommy Hayes and followers of his Cuckoo gang.

But in the Smith case, everything went wrong. The victims should have been Carl and Bernie Shelton. They had been invited to a business conference at Smith's joint by Hayes and Carroll, who were prepared to kill them and take over the Shelton's lucrative bootleg liquor operations.

Carl and Bernie were tipped off by a friendly taxi driver as they alighted from their car near Smith's place at 330A East Broadway. They kept the appointment all right, but instead of being the victims, they rushed into the speakeasy with machine guns blazing. Carroll and Kaminski were shot down on purpose. Hoffman happened to be sitting in the wrong place at the wrong time.

The story of how Carl Shelton played ball with Hayes during the 1930s in order to destroy the power of the Cuckoo gang led by Herman Tipton, was outlined with tremendous force on the Kefauver Committer's crime chart.

Carl Shelton, for almost 30 years the leader of the gang that bore his name, won his battles not by bravado alone, but usually by delegating someone else to pull his chestnuts out of the fire. While he waged territorial war with rival gangster Charlie Birger in the 1920s, Shelton protected his back side by entering into an alliance with the Cuckoo gang of St. Louis. The Burger gang was eliminated by 1930 and Shelton no longer needed the Cuckoos, so he ordered them out of Illinois.

The Cuckoo leader, Herman Tipton, defied the directive by operating a large still on the eastern shore of the Mississippi river near Valmeyer, Illinois, in Monroe county. At least 21 murders of the Cuckoo gangsters, and a few people who got in the way, followed. Carl Shelton's security guards had him destroyed swiftly and cleanly.

The shootings started early on the morning of October 2, 1930. Hayes machine gunners fired a couple of hundred rounds into a cabin where guardians of the Valmeyer still lay sleeping. Peter McTigue, Cuckoo muscle man and William E. Boody, a plumber, were killed. Three other guards escaped, two badly wounded.

Hayes was a clay pigeon after setting a trap for the Sheltons at "Wide-Open" Smith's place. He was sought by gunmen on both sides of the river. Shelton executioners caught him in Madison county in April 1932, polished off his bodyguards, "Pretty Boy" Lechler and "Willie G." Wilbert, in Madison and got Tommy Hayes in Granite City. The skeleton of Homer DeHaven, another Hayes gunman, was found later near Horseshoe Lake.

Later, the Sheltons switched from bootleg liquor to labor racketeering to gambling and became prosperous. They had no opposition and their followers grew soft and middle-aged.

Frank (Buster) Wortman, who had been a minor Shelton hoodlum, must have made some important connections while serving a stretch in Alcatraz for assaulting a prohibition agent. With Elmer Downing, a north St. Louis gangster, and some of the old Egan gang, who completed federal prison terms about the same time, he opened a St. Louis agency for the old Al Capone syndicate.

Led by Jake (Greasy Thumb) Guzik, the Chicago crowd later came to life with the booming gambling business. Gangsters, heavy contributors to campaign funds, were offered almost statewide political immunity in Illinois and they rose to the occasion. The Capones had northern Illinois but the Sheltons blocked them downstate.

Wortman or his mastermind read carefully the first chapter of Carl Shelton's success story and began splitting asunder the Sheltonn's organization. He talked to southern Illinois gangsters, Monroe (Blackie) Armes of Herrin and

Charley "Black Charley" Harris of Fairfield into quitting the Sheltons, although Harris had already done so.

At Chicago the resurgent mob was taking over the national racing wire service after killing James M. Ragen, the former boss. Wortman and Dowling began moving in on Beverly Brown and William (Gully) Owen, the old Cuckoo gang bondsman, who had operated the Pioneer News Company, the local racing wire outlet for years.

Meanwhile at Herrin the seed s of discontent, which Wortman had sown in the Shelton gang, began to bear fruit. Ray Walker, Shelton lieutenant who refused to switch allegiance, was shot and wounded. Walker's cousin, Thomas Propes, was killed after fatally wounding "Blackie" Armes. Ray Dougherty, Armes' cousin, who had been a Shelton gangster in the 20s, was murdered. After the din of all this shooting died away "Black Charley" Harris and Roy (Tony) Armes, "Blackie" Armes youngest brother, emerged as the strong men.

Gangland guns also began silencing a group of hardboiled safecrackers and big time burglars, most of whom had been friendly in a mercenary way, while the Sheltons could be counted on to hire out as bombers or killers for anyone with the cash.

At first they lived at the Arlington Hotel across from the City Hall. The hotel proprietors were Mr. and Mrs. Art Newman. It was said that this wasn't your ordinary hotel. It was also a popular brothel which was operated by Art's wife, Bessie Newman. A short time later the Sheltons moved from the Arlington to the Savoy Hotel across the street. Art later said it was because the Sheltons made it a habit of cleaning their guns in the hotel lobby and Bessie put her foot down. It was scaring away her customers and Bessie hated the Sheltons, anyway, but they still remained friendly with Art.

At one time Art had also been a coal miner, around

Gillespie, Illinois but he and Birger had been partners in crime long before the Sheltons came along.

Charlie Birger was a soft-spoken man of Russian-immigrant parentage who liked children. He was a handsome man who had a passion for silk shirts and silk underwear. Birger was born in Russia but his parents came to America and ultimately settled on a farm near Harrisburg, Illinois, the seat of Saline County, where Charlie grew up. He later served in the U. S. Cavalry.

Birger became the leading bootlegger in the county and drew young boys into his gang, paying them fifty cents or a dollar to steal cars he needed for rum-running.

People around Harrisburg said Charlie Birger always worked within the law but it might be closer to the truth to say he bought off the law.

When John Small was elected Saline County sheriff in 1922, Birger sent an emissary to negotiate the usual treaty. Sheriff Small said the go-between told him he could make seventy-five thousand dollars if he'd do what Birger told him. But he told the agent to tell Birger that, if he bootlegs and makes a million dollars, it's all his but if Small catches him, the law will take its course. Small did catch him later and, as he previously stated, the law took its course . . . Birger went to jail.

When Charlie got out he admitted to Sheriff Small that he had tried to buy him out, but he told him he was leaving Saline County now and wouldn't come back as long as Small was sheriff. He also promised not to let any of his boys kill anybody in Small's county. With that, Birger moved over to Williamson County and opened a roadhouse called the Shady Rest.

By now Art Newman had signed on with the Sheltons who decided to open their own roadhouse north of Herrin in the same county. The gamblers and bootleggers were lacking in leadership, including brains and guns and, what was now the Birger-Shelton gang, provided both. In some of the areas Birger owned the politicians; in others the Sheltons owned them. Some of the sheriffs co-operated for the money while others did it to survive. In the process, the gang became so strong so quickly that the local officials were totally unable to keep up with them.

For years the hill country south of Marion was the home of barefoot hill people but with the end of World War I, the area was now being industrialized and hard roads were connecting Williamson, Saline and Franklin counties. Various workers and war veterans were coming into the area where the pay was good. The gang picked up local guys like the Armes boys and Ray Walker. Later on, Walker would develop into their most valued lieutenant.

Since local feuds back in the 1870's, Williamson had been known as "Bloody Williamson County" and in 1922, Herrin gave the name new meaning as striking miners killed 22 strike breakers in what became known as the "Herrin Massacre". A grand jury brought in a total of 434 indictments but not one person was convicted.

Carl Shelton remarried around 1922, this time to a St. Louis girl by the name of Margaret Bender.*

Could her name have been Mary Margaret with the maiden name of Bender, and the married name of McDermott before she married Carl?

---

* (Footnote: There are two sources with different names for apparently the same woman. The Margaret Bender named in this Chapter, is the name given in the Shelton family records in Wayne County of Carl's second wife. But in the testimony of a man named Renard McDermott, in August 1948, McDermott stated that he was Carl Shelton's step-son, and the son of Mary McDermott who had been married to Carl Shelton until she died in 1932.

In May 1923, the Ku Klux Klan came into Williamson and Saline counties and signed up around 4,000 members. The local people thought of the Klan as a frontier vigilante society rather than a white-supremacy league. The citizens wanted law enforcement and it looked to them like the Klan might do what the corrupted politicians couldn't, or wouldn't, do: clean up the bootleggers and gamblers. It seemed to them that Sheriff George Galligan of Williamson County and other local lawmen were reluctant to take on the bootlegging and gambling element, which was the Birger-Shelton gang.

But the Klan lacked leadership and the Williamson County Law and Order League, which was dominated by the KKK contacted Governor Len Small. At the time the governor had his hands full building a hard road system in Illinois and wasn't in a position to take on this problem as yet. He told the league to elect a sheriff who would agree to take on the problem of enforcing the law.

But the League members weren't about to take "no" for an answer. They went to Washington D.C. but, again, with little or no results. Their trip wasn't fruitless, however. It was there they met a former Prohibition officer named S. Glenn Young. He was born in Kansas and lived a cowboys life and was considered fearless and a crack shot. He was also said to be a former Texas Ranger.

During World War I he was an agent for the Bureau of Investigation branch in the Department of Justice. Then in 1920 he became a special agent in the Treasury Department's newly organized Prohibition Department and assigned to southern Illinois. But in a raid on a house with a still in Madison, Illinois, Young shot and killed a man living next door. He was originally exonerated by a coroner's jury but being a federal officer the case was again tried in the federal court in Springfield where he was again found not guilty. The Prohibition Unit, however, suspended him until they did their own investigation. He was ultimately acquitted but, by then, Young was out of a job!

Some of Young's past tactics were questionable but the Willimson County Law and Order League was desperate for someone who had the guts and leadership ability to clean up the County so, in November 1923, S. Glenn Young came to Williamson County to be the Klan leader.

On January 8, 1924, S. Glen Young led his Klansmen on a raid of Herrin in a cleanup campaign. They "arrested" around 35 men and Young announced that his raids would continue. This began an open warfare with the Birger-Shelton gang.

For the next few months the Williamson County coroner held inquests with verdicts in 153 cases of death. All of them were listed as either deaths from "unknown causes" or death by "person or persons unknown" and another "Bloody Williamson County Massacre" was in progress!

Art Newman said Young and Constable Caesar Cagle led the Klansmen in a raid on the Shelton roadhouse, wrecked the place, and pistol-whipped Earl Shelton in the process.

Street warfare broke out in Herrin on February 8th between the Klan and the bootleggers. Constable Cagle was killed and the mayor and sheriff, who were friends of the Sheltons, were "arrested" by the Klan. The coroner's jury reported that Cagle was killed by "one Shelton, described as tall and slim, and one Shelton who was heavy-set and sleepy-eyed."

Art Newman, who was a Shelton gang member at the time, later said that Earl Shelton and Jack Skelcher came upon Cagle in front of the Jefferson Hotel in Herrin and that Earl walked up to Constable Cagle, pulled his gun and said, "Stick 'em up, you dirty louse." Art said as Cagle raised his hands Earl said, "Oops, too late," put the gun to Cagle's ear and fired. But another version of this incident was described later.

Newman stated that the Sheltons decided that this was a good time to take a trip down south in fear of reprisals from the Klan. He said that, along the way, they held up roadhouses and gambling games as they traveled. But they finally decided they had a better chance with the law than with the Klan, so they came back and surrendered to the law.

The Herrin court house was heavily guarded during their trial, but the jury decided there wasn't enough evidence to convict them. The charge that Carl and Earl had killed Constable Cagle was dismissed.

That afternoon, four blocks from Herrin, a pitched battle broke out and the Sheltons, having been released, were a part of it. Six men were killed and five were wounded. One of the wounded died later. Sheriff George Galligan was seriously wounded and one of the dead was an innocent man who was walking down the street with his wife and baby. A bullet had gone through his head.

The fight had started when Sheriff Galligan went to a garage to seize a car that had been used in an attempted murder of S. Glenn Young. Some anti-Klan boys chipped in $3,000 to go to the man who killed Young. Newman later said the Sheltons weren't doing too well at the time and needed the money.

On the afternoon of May 23, 1924, Klan leader Young told a crowd that had gathered on a Herron street that he was going to East St. Louis to clean up that town, too. The Sheltons were said to have been in that crowd and followed him.

Young and his wife sped out of town in their Lincoln and, according to Newman, the Sheltons had a hard time catching up with them in their smaller car. With the Sheltons were Charlie Briggs and Jack Skelcher. They caught them on a lonely road at Okaw Bottoms. Bernie was driving the car when they opened up on Young and his wife with pistols and a 30-30 rifle. The cars locked bumpers and then the Young car plunged down a bank. Young fell out an open door and crawled under the car, where they shot him and left him for dead. His wife was also shot in the head and face. They both survived but Mrs. Young was blinded.

The next day Klansmen caught up with Skelcher and Briggs; killing Skelcher and wounding Briggs. Carl and Earl were arrested for shooting the Youngs.

Again, the grand jury voted 13 indictments against the Sheltons, including charges of murder, assault to murder with guns and blackjacks, conspiracy and rioting but, for whatever reason, none of these cases were continued. It was said that the Sheltons received part of the money put up by the hoods, even though Glenn Young survived.

The year 1924 was an election year and the Klan was fighting for political control. In the meantime, the Sheltons dropped out of sight. A Marion oldtimer later said, "They indicted pret' near everyone made an ugly face at 'em. It was pretty bad around here. They'd get a Ku Klux grand jury and people'd swear to anything. We didn't have no law."

With the Ku Klux Klan growing stronger, the Sheltons laid low, but not for long. On Saturday morning, September 27th, three men with guns walked into the bank at Kincaid, a coal town near Springfield, Illinois, while three confederates stayed in the car. There was nearly $8,000 in cash on the counter and another $60,000 in the vault.

During the holdup, the bank president began shooting and set off the alarm. One of the hoods hit him on the head with his pistol. Another forced the assistant cashier to put the money into a satchel, but by this time townspeople had arrived with guns. The robber who was carrying the money came out and was shot in the right leg by a grocer. All the money was recovered but several citizens identified Carl, Earl and Bernie Shelton as the bank robbers.

The Sheltons returned to Williamson County that winter and the Klan leader, Glenn Young, was killed by a deputy sheriff in the European Hotel cigar store in Herrin. With Young dead, the Sheltons and Birger could now operate freely. Art Newman sold his hotel in East St. Louis and joined them in Williamson County.

Chapter 3

The Beginning of Another

"Bloody Williamson County War"

Carl Shelton, along with Charlie Birger, Art Newman, Blackie Armes and others, met at Birger's Shady Rest roadhouse on April 13, 1926. It was the day before election and they where planning to go to Herrin the next day to vote for their own people. They also were planning to kill anyone guarding the poles, be it the Klan or anyone else.

A witness who saw them come in, later told a coroner's jury, "I were talking to a lady, happened to look towards the hospital, I saw a string of cars coming, said wonder what that means, couldn't be a funeral; passed along, the men driving slow looking, the first car I saw a gun sticking out, naturally knew what it meant."

A constable who was driving voters to the polls counted six carloads of men. Over forty gangsters were in the caravan and they were looking for Constable John W. Ford. They found him at the Masonic Temple and the leader, who was thought to be a Shelton said, "Go get him," and his men ran at Ford, who later testified, "One of them took my gun with thumb and forefinger . . . I said to him 'Buddy, that's all I have got; I was sworn in here today as special constable to preserve peace.' He said 'Hell you are.'"

With this he took two steps back and began firing at Ford. A friend of the constable killed the gunman but the friend was also killed. Another gunman was shot out of the rumble seat of Birger's sports coupe. Ray Walker put him in another car and drove away.

One of the Shelton boys, probably Carl, was said to be sitting next to the driver in a big car that was blockading the street near the European Hotel, directing maneuvers while Bernie Shelton was shooting. One witness said, "I seen a young fellow shooting out of the window in the west end of the European Hotel, judge he fired fifteen or twenty shots maybe, out of that window; taken aim, fired like a fellow shooting at a squirrel. Other fellows seemed to be shooting pretty well at random . . . Shelton seemed to really be advising the other fellows or dictating as to how they should do, quite a bit of talking . . . This one fellow come over to the side in which we were standing on, told us to stand back in an orderly way, 'You people stand back, no use to commit suicide, be a stray bullet hit you' . . ."

He also said that Blackie Armes "must have been pretty thick with them, seemed to be one of the big leaders." Another witness said that one local gunman was "right in the middle of the bunch down here by the European, had one of the largest guns, seemed to be having one of the best times of his life."

Another witness said, "I stood there about twelve minutes, couldn't talk to nobody, account of so much noise from the guns, and all at once they seemed to have stopped about as quick as it started. They came back to the European, up through the middle of the street, all the fellows went direct to automobiles, throwed their guns in, didn't hesitate at all, got right in the cars, I counted eight automobiles.

"I had seen gangsters patrolling the street . . . I never seen any money exchange hands, but the way I summed it up, there had been quite a bit exchanged hands."

Finally, another local said that the militia came up from the west and the gangsters left. The gang had killed three while three of their own men had been killed. But the gang had broken the back of the Ku Klux Klan and now they controlled the entire area.

That spring the Sheltons and Birger bootlegged without opposition and Williamson County remained peaceful. But it wasn't long until the historic feud began between the Sheltons and Birger.

Art Newman later said the relationship between him and Carl Shelton had begun to deteriorate and about two months later a man named Charlie Gordon was induced by Carl to pick a fight with Newman in Shelton's tavern, in the hopes of killing him. But Newman killed Gordon instead and was indicted for the murder. He was acquitted on the grounds of self defense.

Art then sold the Arlington Hotel and worked out of Memphis, bootlegging and operating some gambling.

Meanwhile, he said, the Sheltons had started a rumor that he had robbed and dynamited a moonshine still in Madison County. This complicated things. He now not only had to watch out for the Shelton boys, he had to also look out for irate moonshiners. So, as a matter of self protection, he decided the only sensible thing to do was to join forces with Charlie Birger, who was already at odds with the Sheltons. Freddie Wooten, a former night clerk at the Arlington, also joined Birger's gang.

The first public indication of a rift between the Sheltons and Birger was in a local newspaper item that describing an armed stranger who was found slain near Herrin. It stated that he was a young man of medium height and dark features, wearing a cap purchased in St. Louis.

It is not generally known why the Shelton-Birger feud began. Birger had said he wanted to bootleg under official sanction while the Shelton boys wanted to hold up people. They obviously aggravated things when they held up one of Birgers friends in Harrisburg, Birger's own hometown.

But Earl Shelton didn't agree with Charlie's explanation. He said the problem began when Birger falsified the gang's account books and took out more than his share.

Most people, however, thought the feud was simply a quarrel over territory; that Birger wanted to move into Willaimson County and the Sheltons wanted to move into Saline County.

The gang members had to chose one side or the other so, in August 1926, Art Newman dropped the Sheltons and became a partner with Birger.

Neither side won the Shelton-Birger "war" and both sides suffered financially as well as physically. Both gangs were operating roadhouses and gambling joints and the battle got in the way of normal business. They got so busy shooting up each other's joints, customers were afraid to visit either place.

It was said ammunition alone cost Birger about $50 a day and he also had to feed about 25 mob members. Art Newman later related that he personally had about $25,000 in the bank when he jumped from the Sheltons to Birger. This was money he had saved up but, by the time the gang war ended, he was broke.

Birger's Shady Rest was a log-style building with sheet metal covered walls. The grounds had been strung with electric lights to protect against night raids. It stood back a few yards from the hard road between Marion and Harrisburg in a wooded grove. A small building in front had formerly been a hamburger stand but now became a guard house with someone always on duty.

The main building consisted of a barroom, craps tables and sleeping quarters and there was a "cock pit" in the back where customers bet on rooster fights. The gang had target practice each afternoon, while evenings were spent doing road patrol. This included knocking over other roadhouses while looking for Shelton gang members.

One of Birger's big money-makers was to mix alcohol with water, then coloring it and putting any label the customer wanted on it. Some even said he used a rusty pipe to color the booze. It sold for $4.00 a pint.

After Birger and the Sheltons began feuding in earnest, Shady Rest was closed to outsiders and Charlie's men would fire at the cars of strangers, which obviously didn't help business.

While all this was going on, Carl Shelton had a home in East St. Louis and the brothers made it their headquarters. Although the Sheltons had fewer men than Birger, they had several hideouts in the area and they kept adding to their gang.

The gang war thoroughly confused the public officials. Now they didn't know who to protect. While the Birger gang began doing highway robbery and such, the Sheltons again laid low and planned ways to eliminate Birger so that they could take over complete control.

In addition to bootlegging, both gangs were deep into gambling. Before they had split up they had mutually controlled every slot machine in southern Illinois.

Early in the war two Birger men, Everett Smith and Harry Walker, were killed by the Shelton gang. Then, on the night of September 12, 1926, three friends of the Sheltons; Max Pulliam, his wife and Bill Holland, were leaving a Herrin roadhouse when their car was riddled with bullets in retaliation. "Wild" Bill Holland was killed and Max was seriously wounded.

Two days later an ambulance, which doubled as a hearse, was transporting the wounded Max and Wild Bill's corpse from the Herrin hospital to Benton. Several cars followed, including one driven by Mrs. Pulliam, giving the illusion of a funeral procession, in case their enemies were watching. As they neared Benton a car sped past which contained a group of Birger henchmen headed by Steve George. He yelled to the driver of the hearse, "Who's dead?" When the driver failed to respond, George fired a few shots at the vehicle then speeded up and blocked the road in front of them. When George opened the rear door of the hearse, there sat Max Pulliam with his arm in a sling, along with a gambler with one of his lady friends. Before George allowed the hearse to leave, they pistol-whipped Pulliam.

Four more gangsters were later killed, but now it was becoming difficult to know which side anybody was on.

Chapter 4

"Armored Wagons" Enter the War

In 1926, the Sheltons were unhappy, to say the least, with Art Newman's decision to jump ship from their gang to Charlie Birger's.

Shortly after that Art and his wife, Bessie, were heading for Birger's Shady Rest roadhouse in a stolen car. Art looked in his rear-view mirror and saw what appeared to be a tank-like vehicle with guns sticking out on either side. Suddenly their car was being riddled by gunfire. Art swerved his car but the lumbering war-like machine following them was unable to negotiate the move, which probably saved their lives. Bessie was slightly wounded while Art was unhurt. But this incident left little doubt that a war between the two gangs was definitely underway.

As it turned out, the "tank" that attacked the Newmans, was a gasoline truck the Sheltons had previously used to haul booze. Birger immediately decided he'd better look for better protection from this kind of warfare, so he had Tom Kane, a Harrisburg cabinet-maker, construct an armored car of his own.

Kane stripped down an old Reo car of Charlie's to its chassis, and armor-plated it. This operation took several weeks and some of Charlie's boys would drop by from time to time to see that the progress kept moving. They often brought "Connie" Ritter along, who was one of Birger's lieutenants.

Some time back Ritter had gone broke operating a shoe store in Marion and Birger made him a once-in-a-lifetime deal. He gave him a big amount of money to handle the financial business of the gang. He didn't have to become "one of the boys" or even carry a gun, He'd just be a white-collar businessman to keep the books and handle the money end. But what Ritter failed to realize was, once you worked for gangsters, there was no way to separate when things got hot.

The Shelton's would later use this same method with a Peoria businessman when they moved to that town. They must have gotten the idea from Birger.

After Birger's armored car was rebuilt, both gang's now had a "war wagon" and these two vehicles became famous in what became the legendary "war" that developed between the two mobs.

On October 4, 1926, Birger paraded his armor around Harrisburg while the Sheltons did the same in Marion. Ten days later Birger's gang machine-gunned the roadhouse of the Sheltons.

Battles began taking place across the hard road between the two towns, to the point that the local folks would avoid using the road. But later, since the hoods carried their guns out in the open to protect themselves, the local citizenry began carrying guns too.

Art Newman later said that one night they were sitting around trying to figure out how they could find Carl Shelton when someone came in and said the Sheltons were at another nearby roadhouse. They jumped into the armored car and a second car and rushed over to that place and "shot hell out of it" with four machineguns plus rifles and shotguns.

"Then," Art said, "they kicked in the door only to find the place was deserted, so we carried out 15 gallons of whisky and wrecked the bar."

As the gang war kept on, both gangs could see that their "war wagon" battles were not getting them anywhere so, after a while, both factions dropped the whole idea.

Birger planted a story in the *Harrisburg Daily Register* blaming the Shelton gang for attacking Art and Bessie Newman and he also told reporters for the *St. Louis Post-Dispatch* stories about the Shelton gang.

Charlie told them, "Sure I'd kill him if I see him, just like he'd knock me off if he'd get the chance. But he's afraid of me, the yellow skunk." Birger claimed he telephoned Carl Shelton in East St. Louis to come down and shoot it out but Carl never came. "And he's got a crowd of red-hots, too, a bunch of professional trigger pullers and roughnecks. All I've got here is a lot of my friends."

Earl Shelton, who was reported to be sick in East St. Louis, disclaimed this story in the *Post-Dispatch* with his own statement.

"To begin with, let me say that this is the first statement of trouble in Williamson County ever made by the Shelton boys, for the Shelton boys do not talk. No, we are not given to boasting of what great warriors we are, like Birger, who is not a warrior but a coward." Big Earl said Birger killed "Wild" Bill Holland, a Shelton man. He described Holland as "a young miner, the main support of his widowed mother and sister . . . a dear little mild-mannered chap . . . This awful crime shocked us all.

"Birger was a good fighter against the kluckers when we were with him, but he never stood alone and he never will . . . I never hurt anyone who did not molest me, and neither have my brothers . . .

"If the state authorities are interested, they will find that Birger has two 'hot' cars, on one of which there is a reward of $1,000 for its recovery."

Earl said that Carl and Bernie, had gone to Hot Springs "for their health" and, "We are not going back to Williamson. There is too much shooting around there, and we invariably get the blame for all of it. Birger can have the war all to himself."

The Sheltons did leave Williamson County, but just to the north of it, in Franklin County, where they set up headquarters in West City, a reputed wide open town.

That September, a fire had consumed an abandoned farm house in southwestern Williamson County. It was being used as a barn to store broom corn. People who were watching the fire believed there may have been a body in it and, after the fire, authorities confirmed their suspicions. They found a belt buckle with a "W" on it. Later, three men went to trial for the murder of Lyle "Shag" Worsham.

Early on the morning of October 26th, a Ford coupe that was riddled with bullets was found parked off of a country road near Herrin and, close by, was the body of William McQuay, also known as "Highpockets."

In the *St. Louis Post-Dispatch*, Art Newman later talked about this incident and several others. He stated that the Sheltons had heard that "High" McQuay, a friend of Birger, was attending the Hippodrome theater in Herron with his girlfriend. The Sheltons told the doorman to bring McQuay out to them at the front door but, suspecting trouble, the two left by the theater's back door. McQuay then headed down the road in his car and, about three miles away, his enemies caught up with him and killed him.

At about this same time two small boys saw a human foot sticking out of the water in Saline Creek near the town of Equality, 25 miles from the Shady Rest. The authorities dragged the body out and it was identified as Ward "Casey" Jones a Shady Rest bartender. His body had been riddled by a machine-gun. It was stated that Charlie Birger paid $498 for Jones' funeral.

Nothing happened in McQuay's death, but the killing of Worsham and Jones resulted in two trials and a hanging.

The Birger gang's plans to get Carl Shelton were speeded up. All three of the Shelton "boys" were becoming hard to find and Birger's outfit listed them as Number 1, Number 2 and Number 3 on their hit list. Carl, as the ringleader, was Number 1 of course. But Bernie, because of his rough reputation, was considered Number 2 and Big Earl was Number 3. The reason Birger's boys attached numbers to them was because they needed to discuss things over the phone, so they began referring to them by number instead of name as a code.

Birger came up with a plan to lure Carl Shelton to the Weis Hotel in East St. Louis and trap him there and they used Carl's old girl friend as a decoy. They brought machine-guns along to rub him out. But the girl friend told her mother about it. Her mother liked Carl and she tipped off Number 1.

Number 1 and Number 2 were becoming increasingly hard to find these days but Number 3 was a "sitting duck" because he, "Big" Earl, was lying sick in St. Mary's Hospital in East St. Louis with malaria.

Now Art Newman and Freddie Wooten decided that the easiest way to reduce the number of Sheltons would be to eliminate Number 3.

Both men were small in stature so they decided to disguise themselves as women to get inside the hospital and then get Earl. Newman put on women's clothes and wore makeup on his face. He didn't change shoes because he was to wait in the car, while Freddie and a henchman went in to get Shelton.

Art and Freddie were later interviewed in the *Post-Dispatch*. Art said, "I wore a swell cape, made of Russian Kolinsky that cost $1,200. Freddie, he was dressed a lot classier. He had a Hudson seal fur coat, a black turban, silk dress, and women's shoes and stockings. He only wears a No. 4 shoe. He had a good clean shave and he was painted up so you'd never recognize him."

Freddie added, "And you remember, Art, I wore a fur neckpiece, or choker, or whatever you call it, but I had to take it off, because I figures there might be some shooting to do and I knew if my rod got tangled in that thing, I'd probably kill myself. We had a lot of fun getting dressed up that night."

They took along Rado Millich, a hired killer, who planned to use a razor-sharp hunting knife to do the actual throat cutting on Earl. This would be noiseless as opposed to having a gun go off in the quiet hospital.

When Art drove up, Freddie got out of the car and walked up to the hospital's front door. In a soft high-pitched voice, he asked the nun at the front desk where "she" might find a Mr. Earl Shelton. When she told him, Freddie said he nearly fell over. "That big boob was booked there under his own name," he said. The "ladies" thought they now knew why Earl was ranked Number 3 instead of Number 2.

But just as they got near "Big" Earl's room, Earl's wife and another woman came out of his room. This gave them the idea that the real women might lead them to Carl's hideout, so they decided to follow them instead.

Earl's wife and friend never led them to Carl, so they decided to go back to the hospital the next day to finish the job but, before they could get back, St. Louis detectives got wind of the plan and nabbed Art and Freddie, along with Art's wife, Bessie, and Rado Millich for questioning. Millich was returned to the Chester jail for breaking parole and Freddie was fined $100 for carrying a concealed weapon, while Mr. and Mrs. Newman were held as suspects.

In the meantime Earl had recovered and was released from the hospital.

Chapter 5

Sheltons add Airplane & Bombs to the War

In mid-October of 1926, Charlie Birger told West City's 300-pound mayor, Joe Adams, that he was going to kill him. He also made the threat public stating it in a newspaper interview. Adams was friends with the Shelton boys, so he made an appeal to them to protect him. They were not only happy to help a friend but this also gave them a new location from which to operate.

There was a rumor that the Sheltons "tank" had been left in West City, and it was thought it could be in Joe Adams' garage. Whether it was true or not, Birger thought the mayor could retrieve it for him, and he threatened to kill him if he didn't. Apparently Birger had also told Mrs. Adams to take out some life insurance on her husband and, sometime later, Joe Adams' home was machine-gunned but no one was injured.

The Sheltons were suspected of alerting the Feds that Birger was selling narcotics and, in retaliation, Birger and Newman tipped off the authorities that the Sheltons had robbed the mails at Collinsville sometime earlier. Politicians as well as other gangsters had also become involved in the plot. A booze runner named Harvey Dungy was picked up by the Birger gang and taken to Shady Rest where Charlie Birger and Art Newman threatened to "rub him out" unless he testified that he had seen the Sheltons in Collinsville the day of the mail robbery, and the next month, Carl, "Big" Earl and Bernie Shelton were indicted for mail robbery.

A short time later an airplane circled Birger's Shady Rest resort. At the time, the only ones there were the caretaker, Steve George, along with Connie Ritter.

From an altitude of about 400 feet, the plane dropped three homemade bombs. One exploded near the road but the only things that were killed was a bulldog and an eagle. Fortunately for Ritter and George, the other two bombs failed to explode.

Then the plane circled back to apparently see what damage had been done. Ritter fired six shots from his rifle, but the plane was seemingly untouched and flew off to the east.

The pilot was later identified as Elmer Kane, a young Iowa aviator. It was rumored that he had been hired by Carl Shelton and paid $1,000 plus an automobile. All three bombs were made out of a bottle of nitro and sticks of dynamite.

Charlie Birger went ballistic because the "war" now included a Shelton "air force" and he commanded two of his gang to kill Mayor Joe Adams.

On December 12, two brothers, Elmo and Harry Thomasson, paid a call to Adams' house and asked Mrs. Adams for Joe. She told them her husband was asleep but they said they had a message for him from Carl Shelton that wouldn't keep and they needed to see him right away.

The sleepy-eyed mayor came to the door and, while he was reading a note they handed him, he was hit by three shots from a .45 and a .38. As he fell from the blasts Joe yelled, "My God, they have shot me." A half hour later West City was without a mayor.

Ray "Izzy" Hyland had been waiting for them in the get-away car, and drove the Thomasson brothers to another roadhouse at Dowell, where they met Art and Bessie Newman and Connie Ritter and his girl friend. They were joined there by Birger and two of his gang, Clarence Rone and Harvey Dungey.

In a later statement of the incident, Newman said that Charlie was "mad as hell" because Connie Ritter had sent "two boys to do a man's job." He felt he should have sent a seasoned gunman who would be less inclined to talk later.

In any event, as promised, Birger paid each brother and their driver, Izzy Hyland, $50.00 for each of the three shots that penetrated Adams' body. Then he, Rone, Dungy and Hyland drove to a roadhouse in Ward, where they were joined by Newman and the others from Shady Rest.

On December 28, Birger was charged with the murder of Adams, even though he hadn't actually done the killing. It had been known that Birger had ordered Adams to be killed but no warrants were served at the time.

During the year 1926, the Birger-Shelton war produced 16 murders, most of which were by the Birger gang. Charlie Birger said, "The Sheltons had not been satisfied to stick to bootlegging and gambling but had turned to bank and highway robberies and whisky holdups. They had been heisting everybody in sight." He claimed that many of the holdup victims were friends of his and, after one holdup, he heard that the Sheltons were out to get him.

But "Big" Earl Shelton's explanation was quite different. He claimed the trouble started when the Sheltons refused to smuggle some of Birger's relatives into the country through Florida. Earl also said, "Later on he (Birger) and I bought some slot machines which he placed in good spots in Williamson County. My brothers and I were to get half the profits. But Birger took it all, and we banished him from the crowd. I told the boys not to have any more to do with him, and that made him wild."

That fall the Sheltons decided to move out of Williamson County for good. Big Earl had contracted malaria and was bedridden for weeks and Bernie went to Hot Springs, supposedly for his health, and Carl divided his time between the two.

A reporter reminded Earl that two of Birger's men, "Casey" Jones and "Highpockets" McQuay, had been bumped off and the Sheltons were being blamed. Earl denied they did it. He also denied the Sheltons had a "gang." He said, "We have friends in Williamson County, who are commonly referred to as our gang," he said, "but we are not robbers or gunmen, but we have never run away from trouble. We don't know if any of our friends are in the fight against Birger, but if they are they will take care of themselves. We are out of it."

In late October, federal officers picked up Art Newman for questioning about the $15,000 Collinsville mail robbery the year before. Both Newman and Birger fingered the Sheltons for it. Newman had still been a member of the Shelton gang at the time. He told the feds he saw the Sheltons dividing a large sum of money.

The federal officers found the Sheltons at the home of West City mayor, Joe Adams, on a tip from Newman and they were later tried for the bank robbery. They were convicted, largely on the testimony of Newman, even though he was known to be highly involved in murder and gambling himself.

About midnight on Saturday, January 8, 1927, Birger's Shady Rest was wrecked and burned. Four bodies were found in the ashes. They had been shot to death and were believed to be three Birger henchmen and the wife of one of them. One of the bodies was identified as Steve George, the caretaker of the Shady Rest.

The fire was blamed on the Sheltons but it later became known that Birger and his lieutenants had removed their valued possessions and all their guns from the place two days before. Also, Birger and Newman had left the building just an hour before the fire, and they were the chief witnesses against the Sheltons.

Birger claimed a state highway policeman by the name of Lory Price had burned Shady Rest and, on the night of January 17, Birger, Newman and five other gang members murdered Officer Price and his wife, Ethel. Newman later claimed that Price knew something about the connection of Harry and Elmo Thomasson, who killed Joe Adams for Birger. He also said, "Birger ordered the murder of Mrs. Price and he himself (Birger) killed Lory Price."

According to Newman, the Birger henchmen had gone to the Price home. Lory and Mrs. Price were there and they asked Price to come out and talk. Price got in the back seat of one of the cars and, as they drove away, Birger called to one of his men to "take that woman out and do away with her."

It was a cold night and raining hard. Newman said they took Price to the recently bombed Shady Rest and Birger shot Price three times as he sat opposite him at a table. Newman said, about that time the other car arrived, and he told Birger, "Here's the other car with that woman and she knows we have her husband." But she wasn't in the car and a man in the car said, "We've killed her." When Newman asked where they put her he said he was told, "In an old mine shaft, just south of the Herrin road." Birger replied, "All right, we'll take Price over there and put him in too." But the other men protested, saying they had filled up the shaft with dirt over her body.

At this point Price groaned. Since he was still alive, they wrapped him in a canvas and put him in the car.

Birger told Newman to sit on him. Price moaned and struggled and Birger ordered the driver to stop. He was sick to his stomach. He told Newman, "I don't know what's the matter with me. Every time I kill a man it makes me sick. Must be my stomach."

Birger ordered one of the men to take Newman's place sitting on Price who was choking and spitting blood and pleading for mercy. When they got to the mine, there was a watchman on duty, so Birger suggested burning Price but it was raining too hard.

They stopped the car near Dubois and Price was hauled out. Newman said, at this point, "He (Price) laid a bloody hand on my shoulder and said, 'Art, I thought you were a friend of mine.' I could feel that hand for months." They carried Price into a field where they filled him with a volley of bullets. It was a week before his body was found.

Mrs. Price's body wasn't found until five months later, when Newman led police to the scene after confessing his part in the killings.

The Sheltons went to trial in Quincy for the Collinsville mail robbery and Birger, Newman and Dungy testified against them. The Shelton boys were convicted and sentenced to 25 years in Leavenworth prison.

Birger was finally arrested in his hometown of Harrisburg but *was allowed to have a machinegun in his cell.* A few days later he was freed on bond.

On a tip, State's Attorney Roy C. Martin of Franklin County found an eyewitness to the murder of Joe Adams and he persuaded one of the gunmen to confess. Birger was arrested and held without bond.

Ethel Price's body was found in the meantime in Williamson County. Birger, Newman and eight other gang members were indicted for her murder along with that of her husband. Birger received the death penalty for Adams' murder and Art Newman was given a lifetime sentence. A Birger gunman was also sentenced to death for another murder and some of the others were convicted of various other crimes.

Harvey Dungy told the Sheltons' attorney and a *St. Louis Post-Dispatch* reporter, John T. Rogers, that his testimony against the Sheltons in the Collinsville mail robbery was false. He said he had been forced to give false testimony under the threat of death by Birger and Newman. And, thanks to newspaper reporter Rogers' further investigation, the story proved to be true and the Shelton boys were freed from Leavenworth and the mail robbery remained a mystery.

While in Menard penitentiary, Art Newman made a statement that, in 1924, the Sheltons held up the bank at Kincaid, Illinois. Carl, "Big" Earl and Bernie were again indicted, and were convicted on January 7, 1928.

But once again a witness changed his testimony and the State Supreme Court reversed the conviction.

Harry Thomasson admitted he and his brother, Elmo, killed Joe Adams at Birger's request, and Charlie Birger, Art Newman and Ray Hyland went to trial in July 1927. Harry apparently decided to talk because Birger had killed his brother when he burned Shady Rest. He also implicated Newman and Hyland but only Birger received the death penalty. Art Newman fled to California but he was brought back and, with Harry Thomasson, was sentenced to life in prison.

On October 7, Birger did receive one stay of execution but, after a sanity hearing the following April, he was found sane and Shachna Itzik, better known as Charlie Birger, was hanged for the murder of Joe Adams at 9:48 a.m. on April 19, 1928.

This marked the end of the Shelton-Birger gang war and the citizens of Birger's home town of Harrisburg cheered wildly in the streets when they heard that Charlie was dead on the gallows.

On January 7, 1929, the rest of the Birger gang were charged with the murder of Mrs. Ethel Price. They pleaded guilty and each received a long prison sentence. The following fall Birger's lieutenant, Connie Ritter, was arrested in Gulfport, Mississippi after a long search. He also pleaded guilty to the murder of Joe Adams and was sentenced to life in prison. Ritter died in Menard Prison in 1948.

Maybe Connie Ritter should have stayed where Charlie Birger found him . . . ***in the retail business, selling shoes!***

Chapter 6

Illicit Profits Where High

But So Were The Costs

Because of the Williamson County war, the Shelton boys' reputations were made after Birger was hung, and they moved back to East St. Louis in the late 1920's with greater power than ever.

The Sheltons had survived six years of murder, robbery, Klan and gang wars, frame-ups and counter frame-ups. They were now big shots in the area. They were held in awe and quickly capitalized on their celebrity.

They did have several run-ins with the law during the late 1920's and early 30's for violating the Volstead Act. Carl served the only complete jail sentence of his "career" by serving 11 months for bootlegging.

The Shelton brothers became wholesale liquor dealers and employed 20 to 30 drivers and guards. The boys were now the biggest operators in Illinois outside of Chicago and, whether true or not, they supposedly had a working agreement with the Al Capone gang.

For years East St. Louis racketeers had operated without interference from politicians or authorities, but now the Sheltons moved in and collected from the gambling houses while giving them "protection" from raids and organized the payoffs. This sounds very similar to what they would later do when they took over in Peoria.

A former southern Illinois sheriff claimed he was offered $1,000 a week to allow just one crap game to operate. On the other hand, a small handbook operator said he only paid the Sheltons $15.00 a week for protection. Big gambling or small, it was estimated that, around 1930, the Sheltons were grossing two-million dollars annually from slot machines, a million-and-a-half a year from horse-race bookers, one-million from other types of gambling and another quarter-million from vice, even though the Sheltons always maintained they never dealt in prostitution or narcotics. All this ran nearly five-million dollars a year, but it didn't even include their lucrative bootlegging operations.

This, of course, was not all clear profit. Even vice lords had numerous costs that had to be covered. For instance; servicing slot machines could run around $110,000, and protection payoffs could go another $300,000 a year. Another $750,000 a year might go as profit to the proprietors who put the slot machines in their businesses. Although this would still leave the Sheltons over $800,000 from slot machines, they would still have to pay salaries to collectors and other employees.

Overall, it was thought all this activity might net them between one-and-a-half to two-million dollars annually, from 1928 to 1932. And this was *really* big money in the middle of the Great Depression!

The Shelton boys had brains, muscle and excellent political connections, not to mention their new found Williamson County reputation, which didn't hurt their operation one bit. A man who knew Carl Shelton well said, "He'd cooperate with the law as far as possible, try to avoid killings and try to be a diplomat. But when he was out to get a guy, he'd get in his car and start out with a shotgun and blow 'im apart."

Even so, Carl was considered generous and loyal to his friends. He neither smoked nor drank. His big weakness was women. One story was that he had three women living with him in his house at one time. He was described as a gentle-mannered man with graying hair who liked to talk. He lived in rich neighborhoods in East St. Louis but what Carl wanted most of all was respect. All his life he had trouble understanding why important men would drink his liquor but wouldn't accept him socially.

Bernie, the youngest of the Shelton brothers, had a reputation of being a heavy drinker much of the time.

One night during one of his drinking bouts, he got into an argument with a working man. He followed him from one saloon to another and waited for him all night. About 7:30 a.m. the man finally left a joint on a motorcycle. Bernie shot at him, which forced him to lose control and slide into the ditch where Bernie proceeded to pistol-whip him.

The man wouldn't prosecute, however. He said, "They won't do anything to Bernie Shelton anyway."

By 1930 the Sheltons began to expand their downstate operations but now they were running into trouble in St. Louis . . . and not just the same old trouble. This time it was with U.S. federal agents.

The country had revived an old 1929 case against Carl, charging him with violating the Prohibition laws. He had violated the Dyer Act by hijacking a $25,000 truckload of, what he thought was booze, but it turned out to be shoes. The judge sentenced him to a year in jail and fined him $500.

While Carl was cooling his heals in jail, Earl was also tangling with the Feds. On July 24, 1931, Earl and two of his gang members, none of whom could swim, were rescued from their sinking boat by Prohibition agents. They used the boat for running booze off the coast of Georgia. Earl was charged with conspiracy and violating the Prohibition and tariff laws.

The year before, a storekeeper named Jerome Munie was elected Sheriff of St. Clair County. He was an honest man who hated the Sheltons. The boys tried to buy him off but couldn't. They knew Munie was Catholic so they tried to win him over by wearing scapular medals when they called on him. Munie didn't buy their act, however, and he arrested them whenever he could.

The Sheltons began putting the muscle on labor unions and Oliver Moore, an important union leader in East St. Louis, claimed the boys offered him $30,000 to move out. After Moore refused, one of them said to him, "Well, Moore, we know where you live." But shortly afterward Moore was shot dead as he left his union headquarters.

As mention before, Bernie was a bully-type when he was drinking and was not above making smart remarks to women who passed on the street and wasn't above pushing teens and their dates around, but Carl didn't want the reputation of interfering with decent citizens. Well, maybe he didn't but Bernie could care less when he was drinking!

In a 1932 reform was on the way in Illinois and Henry Horner was elected Governor. Horner was an honest politician who objected to what was happening in the southern part of his state. In an effort to clean it up, he set up a "Southern Illinois Crime Commission" and put the Shelton boys' old nemesis, Sheriff Munie, in charge. This commission was described as "six fearless good shots with badges" and their assignment: to run the Sheltons and their gang out of East St. Louis.

The boys apparently knew they were through here and Carl's second wife had died in the meantime, so he left East St. Louis and went back to his home in Wayne County to run some farms he had bought.

Meanwhile "Big" Earl was arrested on a liquor charge in Jacksonville, Florida and was sentenced to 18 months in Atlanta prison. After he got out, Earl married Earline McDaniel on April 12, 1936 and settled back on a farm in Fairfield.

Bernie had also married an old girl friend who bought some land on the bluffs south of East St. Louis near where some of the boys had located a moonshine still. She and Bernie opened a dude ranch there, naming it Happy Hollow. Bernie became a good horseback rider and bought and sold cattle and hogs. He stayed on the ranch until his wife divorced him in 1937.

Meanwhile, Carl had already begun putting together another downstate racket "empire." He would go into small towns and force local gamblers to make him a partner. He also had a knack for making deals with politicians in areas that had previously been closed to gambling. Soon his gang controlled gambling up and down a strip of territory running through the middle of Illinois from Peoria to Cairo and, after awhile, the queen city of the Shelton empire became the ***City of Peoria!***

But not right away. He operated in Peoria and Tazewell counties before entering ***"Sin City."***

Chapter 7

Peoria's Reputation Preceded The Sheltons

Back in the later 1930's, there were at least two reasons why Carl Shelton hesitated to enter the town of Peoria, known as "Sin City."

First, "the lid was currently on gambling" and second, he knew of Peoria's past reputation of being, not only a wide open gambling town, but a gangster and vice town as well. This was true for many years, even dating back to before the time the Sheltons started their little games down south. And, after the "Bloody Williamson County" battles, Carl Shelton needed another gang war like he needed "a hole in the head!"

As far back as the 1870's Peoria was known as a wide-open frontier town. In 1872 Wyatt Earp and his brothers, Virgil and Morgan, who became famous gunmen in the gunfight at the OK Corral in Tombstone, Arizona in 1881, lived in Peoria.

Wyatt was born in Monmouth, Illinois on March 19, 1848 at 406 S. Third Street. After his first wife Arilla Southerland Earp died young of typhoid fever in January 1870 in Missouri, Wyatt and his brothers, Virgil and Morgan, moved to Peoria.

Virgil found quarters in a square block of Peoria, infamous for its lewd women and dives called "Bunker

Hill" between Washington and Water and bounded by Clay and Irving streets. He became a bartender there in 1871.

On Feb. 24, 1872, Wyatt and Morgan Earp were seized in a raid on Jane Haspel's brothel in Peoria's red-light district and each paid a fine of $20 and costs. The raid was part of a clean-up campaign launched by a new mayor (who had been mayor previously) T. R. K. Brotherson and his police superintendent, Samuel Gill. Root's Peoria City Directory for 1872-73 listed Wyatt Earp living at Jane Haspel's address on Washington street near the corner of Hamilton. She was a madam and ran a house of prostitution there.

On April 24, a prostitute named Minnie Randall committed suicide by swallowing morphine after she turned state's evidence against the Earp brohers, according to the *Peoria Daily Transcript*. She had been an inmate of the McClellan Institute, another house of ill-repute on Main Street near Water. That "hotbed of iniquity" was raided on May 9 and Wyatt and Morgan Earp were again fined. This time for $44.55. They had no money and wouldn't work so "they languished in Peoria's cold and silent calaboose." The madam of the Institute was Jennie Green. Their fines were now considerably higher, apparently, because the police now considered them "pimps" living in a brothel.

On the night of Sept. 7, 1872, police superintendent Samuel Gill pulled a propeller boat up in the darkness near a 50-foot-long keelboat known to be a floating house of prostitution, moored to the bank of the Illinois River, near Peoria at Wesley Bend, later known as Wesley City. Gill and his officers slipped aboard and he looked in the window. He blew his whistle and his men charged through the doors. The fiddler and dancers scattered but the police shouldered open eight bedroom doors and pounced on the startled inhabitants, including the boat's owner, an experienced pimp from Beardstown. In another room the owner's bartender and right hand-man man was with a roughhouse slugger named Wyatt Earp and a woman named Sara.

The three Earp brothers left Peoria the following year moving west, first to Ellsworth, Wichita and Dodge City, Kansas before moving on to Tombstone, Arizona where, in 1881, the Earp boys entered into the legendary "Gunfight at the OK Corral" with Doc Holliday against the Clanton Gang.

Also before the turn of the century in Peoria, a madam who ran a "home" at Fayette and Washington streets, conducted "Miss Fern's Midnight Cotillion" each Saturday night, which was as well-known as New Orleans' famous "Quadroon Ball."

And after 1929's stock market crash brought on the Depression, Prairie Alley, one of Peoria's "red light" districts also became nationally known, while every house near North Washington and Eaton became a brothel plus many in the near South End.

One well established ten-member gang of bootleggers was the Penn-Julian Gang that was convicted of violating the Prohibition act on December 3, 1929. One of this gang, Phillip Stumpf showed up later during the Shelton era. But this was after he served a jail term related to the previous gang.

He was first arrested in Peoria for robbery February 1, 1929 and was later arrested in Ottawa by the FBI and sentenced to two years and fined $3,000 for violation of the Prohibition Act.

Stumpf was paroled from Leavenworth, Kansas prison on January 3, 1930. Three years later, on February 7, 1933, Chicago police arrested him for robbing a safe and shooting two policemen.

At one time gambling joints were more common in downtown Peoria than banks, restaurants and churches.

One of the best known and most lucrative gambling halls was the Empire Cigar Store at 139 S. Jefferson, offering various types of gambling and the home of the baseball pool, which was said to take in as much as $75,000 a month, paying thousands of dollars for a jackpot . . . and this was in the time of the Great Depression!

But these tough times also brought on another racket that even backfired on the gamblers . . . kidnapping!

Bill Urban, the proprietor of the Empire became a kidnap victim on July 1, 1930, with his seven-year-old-son, Willard. The boy was quickly let go near his home. It's believed Urban paid $80,000 for his own release.

Then on September 15th, Frank Dougherty, the partner and manager of Urban's other "little ball pool" joint around the corner and across the street from City Hall, known as the Alcazar, was kidnapped. He was also later released for an unknown amount.

Information later connected these kidnappings to a gang operating out of Chicago, known as the "Handsome" Jack Klutas gang. Klutas got his start in Peoria, operating his own still and that's why he knew who to target in Peoria and how to do it.

Another attempted kidnapping on the heels of Urban and Dougherty killed the wife of Peoria's "Kingpin" gambler and nearly took his life, too. His name was Clyde Garrison!

Just one month after the Dougherty kidnapping, on October 17, 1930, an attempted kidnapping took place at Clyde Garrison's home, at the corner of McClure and Linn streets.

Clyde and Cora Garrison ate their dinner each evening promptly at 5:30, after which it was their custom to take a drive in their car. A niece of Mrs. Garrison was rooming with them at the time and said she almost went with them on that fateful evening but changed her mind at the last minute as they walked out the back door, or she would have been with them during the kidnap attempt.

Clyde didn't like guns but was usually carrying one these days because of the many kidnap attempts. Cora asked him if he had it with him just before they left. He said no, so she told him to go back and get it.

Clyde put the pistol in his pocket and, just after they stepped out of the back door and were walking toward their car, which was parked in their driveway on Linn Street, the neighborhood was thrown into a bedlam of pistol shots and machine-gun fire.

They had just walked through a grape arbor in the back yard when a man stepped around the corner of the garage and said, "Just stop there Clyde." But instead, Garrison pushed his wife away from him so, as he thought, she would be out of the line of fire. At the same time he pulled his pistol from his topcoat pocket and began firing.

But he hadn't reckoned with another unseen gunman hiding behind a hedge, near where he pushed his wife aside. As Clyde began firing, the second gunman started spraying the area with a machine-gun. Cora slumped to the ground, killed instantly with a bullet through her brain. Another shot entered her right side below the ribs, and passed clear through her body. Two bullets caught Clyde in the right leg and he went down.

In the near darkness, Garrison was unable to recognize his assailants, but he kept firing four or five times and was certain he had hit a man at the corner of the garage. A trail of blood from the yard to Linn Street, where the two gangsters were picked up by a third man driving a car, bore him out. The car moved slowly down Linn Street, turned west on McClure and disappeared.

One of the ironies to this kidnap attempt was that, while waiting for the Garrison's to come out to their car, the gangsters had unknowingly parked their getaway car in front of the home of Peoria County Sheriff, Grant Minor, who lived just two doors up Linn Street from the Garrisons.

Hearing the rattle of the machine-guns, Sheriff Minor laid down his newspaper and stepped onto the porch to listen, followed by his wife. He said, "My God, I wonder if they got Clyde." He dashed into the house to get his gun and during those few seconds his wife cried, "There goes the car." She saw the getaway car stop in front of the Garrison's driveway, and two men got in. One stood on the running board for a few seconds before crawling inside. He was later believed to be the one Clyde hit and, for that reason, was slow getting in the car.

Sheriff Minor got to Clyde just as he sat down at the rear door of the house. Garrison said, "Don't mind me, look after my wife." But a glance told Minor that Cora was dead, and he immediately phoned the Peoria county jail to get his police and deputies onto the hard roads to look for the car.

Afterward, Mrs. Minor said she had noticed a car parked in front of the driveway of their home when she entered their living room after dinner. Another car was parked in front of the residence between their house and the Garrison's driveway. Mrs. Minor later recalled the motor was running in the car nearest their house and she saw it move around the other parked car and pick up the gunmen. She also recalled another car parked across the street which police speculated was probably used to cover the getaway.

About 6:45p.m., fifteen minutes after the shooting, a man standing downtown on Adams Street, waiting to cross Franklin, saw a Packard sedan come racing down the street. Two cars waiting for the green light caused the auto to screech to a stop, then move slowly around to the right between the stopped cars and the curb, and turn south on Adams without waiting. As the big sedan passed him the pedestrian heard a man in the rear seat saying, "My God, hurry along. I can't stand this much longer."

The next morning a buff-colored Packard seven-passenger sedan was found abandoned on the Pekin road between Tuscarora and Hollis. Records showed it had been stolen from its owner, Austin D. Steffner of Chicago, on May 21st, and it still had his initials on the door.

Among other things, several small bloodstains were found on the rear floor, indicating that Garrison had, indeed, hit at least one of the men with his .32 caliber automatic.

Also found in the car was a package containing .45-calber cartridges and a machinegun cartridge clip; a roll of three-inch adhesive tape, suitable for gagging someone; two chains several yards long with snaps and new padlocks; a man's kid glove for the left hand and a man's hat, which had been purchased in Springfield and was believed to have been worn by the bandit that Garrison had wounded.

Also the following morning, a taxicab driver examined photos at the police station in an attempt to identify some mysterious fares he said had him drive around the block of the Garrison home several times the afternoon of the attempt.

Bill Urban, the proprietor of the Empire who had been kidnapped three months earlier, looked at the impounded car and said the dog chains in it were the same kind used to tie him in bed during his capture. But he said two Ford cars were used to kidnap him.

Two nights later a startling event happened. The bullet-riddled body of Charles J. Phayer, a wealthy Madison County gambler, was found along a lonely road four miles south of Edwardsville, Illinois. The police believed that he was the gunman who was shot by Garrison and that his condition was so serious that the gang decided to finish him off. He had already been identified as one of two men seen in the vicinity of the Garrison home a few hours before the attack and an unidentified witness also pointed out four other gangsters as being with Phayer at a downtown hotel that day.

The license plates on the Packard were found to be stolen off another car near an East St. Louis beer joint.

Ultimately four men and four women were picked up for questioning in the St. Louis and East St. Louis area. The four men were returned to Peoria as suspects.

On Monday afternoon, the Wilton Mortuary chapel was filled to overflowing for Cora Rushman Garrison's funeral She was 38. Cora was from Peoria but she was buried in Clyde's home town, Washington, Illinois.

Wednesday morning State's Attorney H. E. Pratt secured statements from the four East St. Louis men: Jack Britt, John "Bad" Moran, Thomas "Nosey" Wilder and Thomas Connors, who were being held in the Peoria County jail, with the questioning being handled by Asst. State's Attorney Leo F. Cavanaugh.

On Thursday Thomas Wilder was pointed out as the one who cut loose with the machine-gun that killed Cora and wounded Clyde. Charles Phayer, who's body was found with 12 bullet holes in it, was identified as the one who ordered Garrison to stand still and was ultimately shot by Clyde.

But suddenly the case went sour.

After several days the suspect's lawyer, John E. Dougherty, demanded that his clients be formally charged or released. Judge Joseph E. Daily agreed, but he also gave State's Attorney Pratt time to develop evidence. But Pratt still didn't bring charges, so the judge released the four suspects.

The *Peoria Journal-Transcript* stated, "Thus, apparently, another unsolved murder is written on Peoria's long list." The paper also pointed out that most of the case work had been done by the Sheriff's office and that the Peoria city police had done nothing "since the night the machine gun rattled."

But the rash of kidnappings didn't stop there. About two years later, on March 14, 1932, Dr. James W. Parker was kidnapped, but was later released when a gang of amateurs couldn't strike a deal.

The Depression days were a dangerous time to live around Peoria for anyone who was known to have big money!

Chapter 8

Hello Carl, Come On In!

Edward N. Woodruff had been Peoria's mayor, off and on, for 11 terms since 1903.

In those early days, a mayor could only serve two years per election until the city ordinance was later changed, allowing a mayor to serve for four years. The change took place when Woodruff was elected his final time, in 1941.

The profane, tolerant old man was called old "crooked neck" behind his back by some of his non-supporters, due to a bad neck that cocked his head permanently to one side. He believed the people wanted a wide open town, and was a champion for the cause when he was in power.

The local gamblers knew this meant "no holds barred" again for games of chance, slot machines and punch boards. Clyde Garrison operated the Windsor Café in the 300 block Fulton street with his partner, Bob McCluggage, the brother of the former mayor, Dave McCluggage, when Woodruff came back into power as mayor in 1941. "Café" was a carry over name used during Prohibition so as not to be targeted as a speakeasy and gambling joint, which it was.

Clyde had been the kingpin of the owners of gambling houses in Peoria in the past when Woodruff would return as mayor every couple years, but this time things were going to be a little different.

For years it had been said that Garrison was the man who brought Carl Shelton to Peoria but, according to a former city detective, who was later on the Shelton payroll, recently said he saw it differently.

Somewhere along the line Woodruff and Garrison must have had a falling out and the "buddy system" between the two was no longer valid. So, when Woodruff told the local gamblers that the "lid" was coming off of gambling in the city again, he told them that someone else would have to take charge instead of Garrison.

John Lucas, a grandnephew of Clyde Garrison, recently indicated that the reason couldn't have been politics. He said his "Uncle Clyde" wasn't a Democrat *or* a Republican. He was for any party in power at the time . . . but if he was anything, he leaned to the Republican side.

Peoria's gambling proprietors met to discuss the problem and were at a loss as to what to do. Past experience told them that someone had to be in charge of payoffs, not only to local politicians but Illinois state politicians as well. But none of them wanted the responsibility and they were at a loss as to naming a new "czar."

Then one of them remembered there was a man out in the Tazewell and Peoria county areas who might be interested. His name was . . . CARL SHELTON!

Carl had been working in the surrounding counties since about 1938 after his gang had been run out of southern Illinois but had deliberately stayed outside of Peoria's city limits for a couple of reasons. First, the lid had been on under previous Peoria mayors and, second, he had recently had a gang-war down south and maybe Shelton just didn't need to fight another blood bath. But now that the mayor, through the proprietors, was ***inviting*** him in, he jumped at the opportunity. After all, it was the first time any city, anywhere, had welcomed him and his gang in with open arms, and the offer was just too good to pass up!

When Carl came north, he brought with him his girlfriend, Pearl Vaughan, from Wayne County. She was a beauty operator and she opened a salon in Peoria, in the old Orpheum Theater building at 116 North Madison avenue. She named her establishment Pearl's Beauty Shop and it was said that all the wives of Peoria's gamblers came there to get their "hair fixed."

It seems obvious that Carl set her up in this business. Pearl also came from Fairfield and was one of the Vaughan clan from the Pond Creek bottoms, the same area from where the Sheltons came.

When Pearl ran this downtown beauty parlor, she lived just a few blocks away, in an apartment house at 804 Hamilton Street.

On April 29, 1943, Carl Shelton and Pearl Vaughan signed a promissory note to George Parks, a partner in the Par-K Club with Frank Kraemer. It was for a $6,000 loan to buy a house at 1308 Knoxville avenue in Peoria.

The stipulation of the note stated that they agreed to pay $75.00 a month to Parks' account at the Jefferson Trust and Savings Bank, beginning June 1, 1943. The interest on the loan was figured at 4%.

The house was purchased on April 29th from People's Federal Savings & Loan Association. The warranty deed did not list the selling price but it showed the sale was made solely to Pearl Vaughan. Carl's name did not appear on the document.

Pearl closed her shop downtown and began operating a beauty shop out of this Central Bluff location, and Carl lived there with her. His Social Security card listed this address and it also listed his business as the Palace Club, in the 200 block South Madison avenue. This club was the headquarters for the Shelton operation in Peoria.

When Carl registered for the draft on April 25, 1942, he signed his full name, Carl Ray Shelton on his Selective Service card. He signed it in Wayne County, Fairfield, Illinois, which described him as white; height, 6'-1"; weight, 210 pounds; eyes, brown; hair, black and gray and complexion, ruddy.

In the early 1940s, a businessman named Harry Tyrrell was a prominent citizen in town who owned several businesses, including the Northern Steel & Stoker Corp.; the Harry Tyrrell Studebaker dealership; Tyrrell's Tiny Tots shop, run by his wife; Peoria Appliance Sales and the Carl Burlings Corporation of Pekin, Illinois.

Tyrrell had also recently gone into partnership with Ray McDaniels in a jukebox business but someone who was in competition with them was applying pressure on the tavern and restaurant proprietors to take Tyrrell's record machines out and putting in their own. Suddenly Harry was losing up to $20,000 in the venture and he had to do something to save the business.

Knowing Carl Shelton's reputation, Harry contacted him and asked Carl if he would like to go on his payroll. Harry figured, if the competition heard that Carl Shelton had an interest in *his* business, they'd leave him alone. Carl agreed to join Harry and the problem stopped immediately.

But Tyrrell apparently didn't know he was playing right into Shelton's hands, because Carl also had a need. He wanted a legitimate businessman to be a chief collector to handle his gambling operation's books, similar to what Connie Ritter had done for Charlie Birger down south. Tyrrell agreed to do this for Carl but it automatically caused Tyrrell to cross the line from legitimate business to illegal gambling.

When Carl Shelton took over in Peoria he didn't come alone. He again used his brother, Bernie, for muscle, along with another brother, "Big" Earl, although Earl never lived permanently in Peoria, and a nephew "Little" Earl, named for his infamous uncle.

He also brought Ray Walker, who was one of Carl's top henchmen during the "Bloody Williamson County War" against Charlie Birger's gang in southern Illinois.

Ray had been a "bad boy" since he was 17 years old. He served a year in the Chester, Illinois jail for assaulting a man in Mt. Vernon. Then he spent over three years in Menard prison for aiding and abetting a jail break and, later, served three years in Leavenworth prison for an assault on a federal officer, in June 1934.

Ray had been a gambler the last ten years, in Fairfield and also in Kentucky. He was usually a craps dealer in dice games. After Bernie Shelton opened a place in Peoria called the "Play Home," Walker worked there until the Sheltons opened the "Palace Club" on South Madison, across from City Hall. This became headquarters for the Sheltons and Walker worked there for "Speed" Harding and Bill Manning, but he left because of the long hours.

Walker maintained he was just a friend of the Sheltons but he had been a member of Carl's gang in the "war" down south. He had also been in business with Carl in Fairfield in craps games for three years. So when the Sheltons moved to Peoria, Carl gave him some slot machines and Ray later said he was running slots for about two years and was given permission to operate by Charlie Somogyi, the chief investigator of the Peoria County States Attorney's office. Somogyi, however, denied he was ever involved in, or cooperated with, gambling.

Part of the time Walker stayed at Carl's home on Knoxville and part of the time in Fairfield, where his wife was staying at Earl Shelton's farm.

Now the Shelton boys not only controlled Peoria gambling, but the surrounding counties as well.

One thing Carl Shelton found to be the same in Peoria as it was in Southern Illinois was a lack of friendships in the business world. Most businessmen would patronize his gambling operations but wouldn't socialize with him. He still had a need for being accepted as a friend, but few were willing to get too friendly, probably for fear of reprisals.

One man who did become a personal friend operated a grocery store in the South End of town. His name was Anthony "Tony" Couri and his store was located at 1101 South Jefferson.

Tony first became friends with Ferd McGrane, who worked for Carl Shelton. Ferd would come into his store and sit on the counter and shoot the breeze with Tony.

One day McGrane told him he had a friend he'd like him to meet. He said he was a wonderful guy and his name was Carl Shelton. So, one day Carl came in with McGrane. He and Tony hit it off right away and eventually became good friends and, according to Tony, never discussed gambling.

This friendship apparently helped fill the void of a businessman's friendship in Carl Shelton's life. Tony Couri became Carl's best business friend which lasted to the end.

During World War II there was rationing of everything from gasoline to meat and groceries. Carl mentioned to Tony that his mother in Fairfield had a favorite soap powder she had used for years but she couldn't find it anywhere.

Tony told him that he received large boxes of it on occasion and, the next time it came in, he'd hold it for Carl's mother. Carl was delighted and never failed to buy his mother's soap whenever his grocer friend called. He also began buying his groceries from his new found friend.

Now, you might think that Carl would suggest to his new friend that he put his slot machines and punch boards in his store, but Couri said the question never came up between them, even after Tony became a partner in another business, Si Maroon's Tavern, on Western Avenue at Main Street.

Although he still operated his grocery store, Tony Couri became a partner with Maroon. It was said Si was in deep financial trouble at the time and was about to go under. Being the smart business man that he was, Tony Couri became a partner with Si and was instrumental in saving the tavern.

Chapter 9

While Carl Made Friends Mayor Woodruff Made Enemies

Pete Petrakos became friends with Carl Shelton, too, but his association became very entangled with the rackets and gambling.

Pete was born on the high seas in 1907 as his family came to America from Greece. They settled in Peoria and after Pete graduated from Manual High he worked for the State of Illinois and became involved in political campaign management.

Out of work during the Depression, he went back to work for his father's ice cream parlor on Perry Street, then got a job at Caterpillar from 1932 to 1938.

His dad was a friend of Loyal Sprague who had a printing press and sold punch boards all over the city. Loyal invited Pete to sell punch boards and he began grossing $250 to $400 a month.

Pete started frequenting Bill DeGaris' tavern across South Madison Street from the *Peoria Star* newspaper buiding. Many of the city and county officials came in there for drinks and lunch and this was where Pete met Carl Shelton. Pete said he never saw Carl drink or smoke and never heard him cuss. Carl would buy him a scotch and soda and a coke for himself.

Another man Pete got to know at DeGaris' was Judge Claude U. Stone, the publisher and editor of the *Peoria Star*. He was always coming to Stone there with a "scoop" for his paper or other information. It soon became known that Pete had built a pretty good friendship with Stone.

Prior to 1902 Claude Stone had been principal of schools in Brimfield, Illinois and from 1902 to 1910 was County Superintendent of Schools in Peoria County, and since 1909 had been a lawyer and then Congressman three times. He also became Master of Chancery of the Circuit Court of Peoria County for 16 years, and was a cousin to Judge Clyde E. Stone.

Petrakos was drafted in 1943 but four months later his father died and he got leave to come back for the funeral. He was later honorably discharged and went back to work for Sprague.

There were few, if any, towns where illegal gambling was as wide open as it was in Peoria in the early 40s. At Mayor Woodruff's insistence, the gamblers paid a slot machine "tax," which went into a special fund in the Peoria city treasury. This "funny money" fund from slot machines alone, took in around $169,000, a tidy sum back then when nickels, dimes and quarters added up as fast as the cherries, oranges, plums, bells and lemons could spin.

There were also payoffs to other local public officials and, once a month, Carl would drive out the hard road toward Springfield, where he parked his car to meet a state official and give him $2,000. It was said this figure later grew to $5,000 or more. Shelton had taken over this job of payoffs at the state level from Clyde Garrison, the previous "czar" of Peoria gambling. Obviously this didn't make friendly chums out of Garrison and the Shelton boys.

But that wasn't the only Illinois State payoff. Another payoff was made in the same manner to Chicago by another messenger for Carl Shelton. His name was George Chiames.

A former Chicago Taxicab driver, Chiames came to Peoria in 1926 and opened a pool hall in the basement of the Peoria Alliance Life building. He soon became influential in the flourishing gambling industry. He operated punchboards and owned a part interest in dice games in Peoria, Tazewell, Mason and Fulton counties in the past.

By the end of 1941, Mayor Woodruff's open gambling policy was becoming quite known within local political circles. The views of Peoria's city council became public the night of December 9th at the council meeting when they voted for the elimination of punch boards in the city and an accounting of "fines." This caused the mayor to explode with an invitation for the council to impeach him if policies of his administration were not satisfactory.

Woodruff charged that their action was an attempt to crucify him. "What is your object in making these things public?" he asked. "I'm shaping the policies of this administration and if people feel we are doing wrong, they can hold me responsible."

William Buchanan, an alderman for the Fifth Ward, presented the council's position under two resolutions. One called for a report on the amount of money gamblers paid to the city in the last six months and when, for whom and by whom, the money was paid.

The other resolution instructed the mayor and other proper city officials to eliminate all types of gambling and games of chance in night clubs. Both resolutions were adopted unanimously.

The mayor replied, "The city has been paid between $17,000 and $18,000 in the past three months, and I don't know where the money came from and I don't care. If you're going for social reform, go to it. If no one likes me, impeach me. These things were going on before I came in and you're pointing them at me. I'm still executive officer . . ."

Buchanan countered with, "You're not the supreme ruler. The only trouble with you, Mayor, is that you are in the wrong company."

Buchanan went on to charge that operators of night clubs were special friends of the mayor and that the men behind them were a bunch of ex-convicts, and he threatened to seek the aid of the city attorney in banning gambling, contending that the city "can find legal money to finance it."

Ninth Ward Alderman William Kumpf, who was also chairman of the finance committee, said he had no doubt of the sincerity of Buchanan's resolution and that he would vote for it, but he also said Buchanan "had gone too far and the mayor did not deserve such criticism."

Sixth Ward Alderman Joseph M. Mittleman moved for the elimination of all punch boards and his motion was adopted after an appeal from the ruling chair, Mayor Woodruff, that he was out of order.

"Why stop there," asked the mayor, "are checkers next?"

Chapter 10

Gamblers Had Their Problems Too!

Things were really heating up in Peoria's city hall but it was not all fun and games with the gambling joints either.

For a time there were a few hold outs around some of the town's "watering holes." Some of the independent gamblers wouldn't go along with Carl Shelton and his gang.

So, one Saturday afternoon, Bernie and some of his "strong arms" paid a visit to one of the "hold out" saloons. The gang proceeded to overturn the bar, throwing the bar stools through the mirror, smashing all the glasses and whiskey bottles on the back-bar and dumping over the cash register.

Somebody called the police but, when they came, they told the proprietor that his bar was causing too much trouble with fights and rough stuff lately. The cops advised him that, maybe he needed a good partner, indicating the Shelton boys.

The defense effort and World War II caused a booming economy in the early 1940s, for the first time since the previous war and following Depression, and the gambling business rode the high wave along with everything else. The Sheltons became highly organized in their new Peoria surroundings and they could scatter the sales of a load of hijacked liquor so fast it could never be traced. They had about 20 men working for them, who also had their little sidelines going.

Carl had a way of knowing what was going on, even if he was down on his Fairfield farm and, if Bernie and his henchmen were wasting time in some Peoria saloon, he'd know it and call the tavern and tell them to pay attention to business.

It's said that Carl spent $75,000 in an unsuccessful attempt to defeat one candidate for office. But the Sheltons were never arrested in Peoria. After all, they had the mayor behind them and they worked with the law because the law worked with them . . . or, better yet, *for* them. One Peoria detective said, "They (the Sheltons) were always running to the cops, the sheriff or the FBI, with tips on every little crime, to hang it on people they were sore at and to integrate themselves with the authorities." Their control of power in Peoria became greater than it ever was in East St. Louis.

Although the Sheltons didn't break up his place, Joe Rafool was operating a tavern and gambling operation in East Peoria called the "Pair-a-Dice Lounge" in the 1940s and, years later, he reminisced with Jerry Klein of the *Peoria Journal Star* about a visit from the notorious gang.

Shortly before noon on a summer Saturday, the Shelton boys walked in, Rafool recalled. They included Carl, Bernie, "Big" Earl, "Little" Earl Shelton and Ray Walker. According to Rafool, Bernie shouldered his way into Joe's little office and said: "Rafool, you got a nice place here. As of twelve o'clock, you got yourself a partner."

In the interview Rafool said: "I gave Bernie the key and said: 'Here, it's all yours,' and I started to walk toward the door. He didn't want it that way. He kept saying, 'Yes, but, but, but . . .' He tried to pull me back. 'I only want part of it,' he said, so I closed up . . ."

Rafool went on to say that, later, the Sheltons and an influential businessman (he refused to name him but it probably was Harry Tyrrell,) ended up owning a major interest in the lounge.

But the story of the disagreement of Joe Rafool and the Shelton gang didn't end there, because Joe did finally change his mind and returned to his Pair-a-Dice Lounge, or, to put it another way, he had his mind changed for him. Joe found out in a hurry it wasn't going to be that easy to separate from the Shelton gang when they had other ideas.

The word went out that the Sheltons put a "contract" out on Joe, meaning of course, that Rafool was going to be killed. It didn't happen though because, when Carl Shelton's friend, Tony Couri, heard about it, he contacted Carl and asked him to spare Joe Rafool's life, which Carl did.

Rafool was still concerned about it, though, and became even more concerned about the safety of his family.

Joe had married a Lebanese lady from New Jersey and brought her to Peoria to raise a family. They had two girls and three boys. So after his run-in with Bernie, Rafool decided it might be a good idea to send his wife and children back to New Jersey for awhile, in case there might still be repercussions about his leaving the club. The family moved back east to Mrs. Rafool's hometown in New Jersey, where she entered the kids in school.

But a short time later Joe received a phone call at his home. A man's voice said he was calling from a payphone across the street from the school where his kids were in class at that very moment.

Joe Rafool immediately returned to the Pair-a-Dice Lounge and became a front man and partner with the Sheltons!

Rafool continued to operate the lounge until after Carl and Bernie Shelton were killed and illegal gambling slowly shut down. Rafool's brother-in-law, George Shady, was a gambling table dealer at the lounge and, one day, one of the employee's asked him about the basket of checks that were always under the bar. Shady told him they were bad checks that Rafool had collected over the years. They amounted to around $70,000 worth of checks that had "bounced" and Joe kept them there to remind him of the old days. Joe also kept another reminder. He still had the original pair of dice that were used when he first opened the lounge.

The Pair-a-Dice continued to operate as a legitimate tavern and finally Joe leased it to George Shady, who operated the, now legal, Pair-a-Dice Lounge until it finally closed years later.

But this is far from the end of the Joe Rafool story. Joe had made a lot of money over the years and was a visionary person. So much so that he ventured into the real estate business and began developing subdivisions in the area.

One of his first projects was developing the subdivision on the west bluff which became the location of St. Philomena's Catholic Church. He moved into the a house on Avalon Place, just across from the church.

He developed a similar project in East Peoria, naming it the Fondulac subdivision which included St. Monica's Catholic Church.

Joe was a smart and shrewd businessman but after the Shelton era, trouble followed him around mainly because of his association with the Sheltons as partners in the Pair-a-Dice.

Apparently the lounge owed a large amount of money in back taxes to the federal government, while he was partners with the Sheltons. It was rumored the Internal Revenue Department claimed the lounge owed about

$300,000 that had never been paid during the Shelton partnership.

Carl and Bernie Shelton had both been killed in the mid-1940s but the government still wanted its tax money and they went after Joe Rafool for the full amount until 1960, even though his partners were long since gone. Joe finally had to pay the entire amount, including the Shelton's cut, which virtually wiped him out. He had to borrow a big part of the payment from friends, which left him virtually penniless.

The tragic end of Joe's career came in the late 1970s. He was still trying to run a one man operation out of a small office in the 200 block of Monroe street.

But Joe was getting older and unable to keep up with the new technology. He was still sending out mimeographed letter's on an old beat-up typewriter to businesses all over the country. Joe was trying to catch lightning in a bottle that he once had going for him, but it never happened. It's a very sad ending to one of Peoria's most successful entrepreneurs of his time . . . but the world had passed him by!

But the Pair-a-Dice Lounge wasn't the only hot gambing casino and "watering hole" in Tazewell County back in the wide-open 1940s.

One place started small on Route 29 between Creve Cour and Pekin. It became one of the hottest stops for gambling, drinks and entertainment in the area.

The place opened in the mid-1930s as the Midway Tavern and included two gas pumps out front and three tourist cabins outside.

After a complete remodeling about 1944 it was expanded and became The Open Door. When the contractor finished the building, he handed the keys to the owner who immediately threw them away. He said he wouldn't need keys because The Open Door would never close, and it never did as long as it was in operation. It operated all day and all night, seven days a week.

It became a favorite entertainment spot with gambling, a floor show, including seven or eight vaudeville type acts three shows a night, every night at 10pm, 2am and 5am. The performers were backed up by a six-piece band directed by Fats Dudley.

The Open Door became another hot spot for gambling and entertainment in Tazewell County and, once again, the Shelton's decided to go into partnership with it's owner as they had done with Rafool, but this attempt backfired on them.

One day three men walked into the place one at a time and set down at the bar. They were identified as Bernie Shelton, Ray Walker and an assistant to the Peoria County state's attorney. The young man tending bar at the time was the younger brother of the owner and they told him they wanted to talk to the boss.

When the owner came out, Bernie informed him they were going to be his partners in the operation. They said the owner could keep the liquor end of the operation and the entertainment, but the Sheltons would take over the gambling casino. The owner asked them what they were willing to pay him for it and Bernie said "nothing." They would just be his partners.

The owner answered, "Over my dead body!" At this point Ray Walker pulled a pistol out of his shoulder holster and said, "That can be arranged!"

But what the three didn't know was there was a 12-guage shotgun under the bar. The bartender reached for it and pulled out the shotgun so they could see the butt end of it and pointed it, from under the bar, right at the belly of Walker, at which point Walker dropped his pistol on the floor. The owner told him he could pick it up and the three men made a hasty retreat.

The following night during the peak of business, a carload of gangsters drove past the Open Door, and shot up it's electric sign and the entire front of the building before driving off.

This probably took place in early 1946 while the gambling casino was in the process of building an addition of a 10-room motel. A few nights later a part of the motel was bombed, which blew up units 8, 9 and 10 of the not yet completed building.

A man named Frank, who acted as a go-between of the gambling joints in the Tazewell area, took exception to what had happened to the casino's motel. He knew it was the Sheltons who were up to their old tricks, reminiscent of the Bloody Williamson County gang war, so he took things into his own hands by going over to Peoria and bombing the Palace Club, which was the Shelton's headquarters. He bombed the area where the Shelton's repaired their slot machines.

The Open Door was one place the Shelton bluff backfired and The Open Door stayed open for business as usual.

But even though the Shelton gang did try to muscle in on any operation they could, Bernie had earlier bought his own tavern legally and was said to have even paid far too much for it. It was the Parkway Inn in the 300 block of Farmington Road.

Before that he had bought an 80-acre farm a few miles further out that same road and named it, of all things, Golden Rule Farm. Bernie liked to ride horses ever since his Happy Hollow dude ranch days south of East St. Louis and, here in Peoria, he raised Palomino horses. At one time he had a string of 30 of these blond beauties. He had also paid $2,750 for a saddle and liked to go to rodeos in Wyoming.

His old remodeled farmhouse was surrounded by landscaped grounds. Its high-ceilinged rooms were dark and cool and he hung etchings of old-time western scenes with cowboys and horses.

The Parkway Inn was owned by a Mr. and Mrs. Betson, who lived in Edwards, Illinois. Bernie had become good friends with the Betsons and he'd go out to their farm and have a few drinks with them from time to time.

On one of his visits he told them he liked their tavern and its location near his farm and asked if they wanted to sell it. But, at the time, the Betsons were making a good living with the place and didn't want to sell, so they turned down Bernie's offer. He must have been in a good mood at the time. Instead of threatening to take it over, he said if they ever changed their minds, he'd like to buy it.

Some time later, the Betsons did change their minds. They weren't getting any younger and were planning to retire. They mentioned the offer from Bernie Shelton to their son, Harold, who agreed that they should see if Shelton was still interested, but he also made a suggestion.

He advised them to decide what they thought would be a fair price and then triple the figure before talking to Bernie. Harold figured if Bernie Shelton wanted the place badly enough, they might not get what they asked but they could always negotiate down and still come out with a better deal.

The Betsons took their son's advice and called Bernie. They told him they were now thinking of retiring and were ready to sell the Parkway and quoted him the inflated figure. To their great surprise Bernie immediately accepted the offer. He said, "Who's your lawyer, I'll buy it right now!"

So the Betsons sold the Parkway Inn to Bernie Shelton for three times what they thought it was worth. Apparently, to a guy who made big money in the rackets, enjoyed Palomino horses and expensive saddles, the price of a tavern was of no consequence.

This had to be the first AND ONLY time Bernie Shelton was ever "held up" instead of the other way around!

On November 26, 1947, Bernie Shelton married Genevieve Tabor, who had been married twice before; first to a man named Paulsgrove and later to Harold Tabor.

Tabor had been a bartender and back in the 1930s he became a partner with Jack Ashby. They operated the 101 Club at 101 Fulton Street, just across from the Rock Island depot.(Ashby later became Bernie Shelton's partner in the Shelton Amusement Company.)

Genevieve was married to Tabor from 1931 to 1940 and was said to be an inmate in a house of prostitution and, later, was the madam of her own "house" in the 400 block of South Jefferson Street.

Jack Ashby had done a little bootlegging during Prohibition and later ran a couple taverns around town after liquor was legalized. He married his wife, Mary, in 1937. She had also worked in a house of prostitution run by Inez Ryan at 229 South Washington Street for five years, until she married Jack.

In 1938 Ashby went into the juke box business with Jimmie Meyers at 210 Hamilton Street. Meyers put up the financing and bought the machines and Ashby, who had experience in radio electronics, was the electrical mechanic and serviced the juke boxes.

It was at this time that Ashby first met Bernie Shelton, who had just come to Peoria from Wayne County. They met at the St, Elmo's Tavern, which was just below Jack's second floor business. Ashby and Myers sold their business in 1941 and Jack worked in defense jobs until he volunteered for the Army Signal Corp. in 1943.

After the war Jack ran into Bernie Shelton again. This time it was at the Mecca Supper Club on Farmington

Road, right next to Bernie's Parkway Inn. Bernie told him he had gone into the "machine business" while Jack was in the service. It was the Shelton Amusement Company with offices right next to the Parkway. (The company was owned by Bernie and Carl.) He asked Jack if he wanted a job servicing juke boxes for him.

At first Ashby turned him down saying that he couldn't make a decent living on Bernie's offer. But Bernie also had some pinball machines in partnership with someone else so he approached Jack again with an offer of servicing the juke boxes and the pinball machines as well. Ashby finally took the job in December 1945.

Shortly afterwards a man named Dentino , who owned 50 pinball machines, offered to sell them to Bernie and this gave Shelton an idea.

Bernie took a liking to Ashby and wanted to keep him, so he offered Jack a proposition. He suggested that they buy Dentino's "route" together. This would make Jack a partner in this legal business and not just an employee. Ashby agreed and later became the manager and bookkeeper of the Shelton Amusement Company.

Bernie also had 18 slot machine locations, which Ashby didn't service at first. But by the end of 1946, he started servicing three slot machine locations in Peoria County.

Just about six blocks out Farmington Road from the Parkway was another place called Murphy's Restaurant. Jack Adams who operated the Clover Club downtown, just across the street from city hall, bought Mrs. Murphy's restaurant and changed the name to the Sportsman's Club. This had been the name of the downtown location, before he changed it to the Clover Club.

Living next door to this newly named club was a man named Roy Gatewood. He was in the process of buying four or five acres of property, which included the land where the new Sportsman's Club and his own home stood. He later bought the Sportsman's Club building from Jack Adams.

Gatewood was also in the advertising business, owning his own firm, the Ace Advertising Company, with offices in the Jefferson Building downtown. He was also good friends with Roy P. Hull, the new State's Attorney of Peoria County.

Gatewood first met Carl Shelton when Carl visited his office and offered to lease the Sportsman's Club to put gambling in a casino upstairs. He agreed to lease the place to Carl but in the meantime something happened and Carl let the matter drop.

Gatewood also said he got into the punchboard business when Roy Hull and attorney Clyde Trager advised him to buy the boards from a local firm, Gamm Sales Company. He bought over 250 boards and said he paid Hull $150 for permission to put them out in Peoria County, but he only sold a few because virtually every joint in the area already had boards, so he gave away the remainder.

In 1946 some friends of Roy's, Mr. and Mrs. Glen Carroll, stopped by his house one afternoon while he was cutting the grass. The three eventually went over to the Sportsman's Club to have a beer. At this time Ben and Irma Jewell were leasing the club from Gatewood. Shortly afterward the Carrolls left with some friends and Gatewood sat a minute to finish his beer. Bernie Shelton, who had been drinking with another man, was sitting at the bar.

When Roy got up to leave, someone had locked the door. At this point Bernie said to him in a gruff voice, "Come here, I want to talk to you." Gatewood knew Bernie's reputation of getting mean when he drank, and walked over to him. Bernie said, "I understand you are picking on my friends here," meaning the Jewells. Gatewood said he wasn't picking on anyone, but Mr. Jewell wasn't paying on his lease and Roy's attorney was taking them to court.

At this point, according to Gatewood, Mrs. Jewell began hitting him on the back and, while trying to push her and her husband away, Bernie hit him with his right fist along the side of his face. Then Bernie opened his coat and brandished a .45 pistol. He swung the gun and hit Roy with it. While Gatewood was trying to defend himself against the three of them, he backed away toward the door and Shelton hit him with his pistol again in the forehead.

In the meantime Mr. Jewell had unlocked the door to go get his .32 pistol out of his car. Roy said, as Jewell came back through the kitchen with his gun, he struggled to his feet and hit Jewell as he backed through the door. Covered with blood, he ran to his house. The Sheriff's department was called but, by the time they got to the tavern it was closed.

The next day Sheriff Swords and his deputy, Gay Duenberry, came to the Gatewood house and asked Roy what he wanted to do about the fight. Mrs. Gatewood was mad and demanded that they get Bernie and bring him to the house, which they did. Bernie, who was now sober, indicated he was sorry and guessed he had been misinformed. Gatewood called his state's attorney friend, Roy Hull, and said, if Hull would swear out a warrant against Bernie, he'd sign it. But Hull advised him not to do it because he and former State's Attorney Carson had been working on getting rid of the Sheltons altogether, and he'd better leave it alone at that.

Chapter 11

Some Family Facts About The Garrison Clan

John Lucas, Clyde Garrison's grandnephew mentioned earlier, said Clyde came to Peoria from Washington, Illinois and John's grandmother was Clyde's sister, Nell Garrison. She married Raymond Bellows, a railroad conductor and they had a daughter, Ramona. When Ramona was three, Nell divorced Bellows. She found he was conducting more than railroad business with the wife of a hotel proprietor in Pekin. She later married Ed Norman and after he died a few years later, she married Tom Tanton, the widower of her sister, Josephine.

Shortly after her divorce from Bellows, however, Nell moved to Chicago, where she wound up owning a small hotel near the famous Edgewater Beach hotel. Her principal income came from a 24-hour poker game and she was the "house." John said she could beat anyone at poker, including Clyde.

When Nell went to Chicago she left her daughter, Ramona, (John Lucas' mother) in Washington with her brother, Clyde, and the Garrison family. They raised "Mona" until she was 15 or 16 years old. Then Mona took off for Chicago to find her mother and lived with her for three or four years.

John Lucas' father, Edwin "Eddie" Lucas was from Washington, Indiana and did odd jobs including being a barnstorming pilot who, at about age 20, wound up in a casino in Detroit as a craps dealer. He came to Chicago and dealt craps at the Tip Top Tap in the Allerton Hotel. Eddie met Mona who was working in a candy shop and they got married.

In the meantime Clyde Garrison was married and living in Peoria. In 1930 when his wife, Cora, was killed and Clyde was seriously wounded in the kidnap attempt, Eddie and Mona came to Peoria and lived with Clyde on McClure and she nursed him back to health. Mona was pregnant with John Lucas at the time and John was born in St. Francis Hospital. He lived with his parents as a new born baby at Clyde's home.

His mother told the story that, at the time Clyde was trying to make friends with an up and coming politician named Everett M. Dirksen. Visiting Clyde one day and, being a good politician, Dirksen picked up the baby, at which time "Baby John" proceeded to wet all over him. She said Dirksen left hurriedly and told Clyde he'd call him Tuesday, but he apparently didn't say which Tuesday, because Clyde never saw Ev Dirksen again. Apparently Baby John had put a "damper" on their friendship!

When Clyde first came to Peoria, he formed a partnership with Bob McCluggage, a brother to the previous Peoria mayor, Dave McCluggage, and they opened a place in the 300 block Fulton named the "Windsor Coffee Shop," a front name for a gambling joint during Prohibition.

Eddie Lucas later ran errands for Clyde, emptying slot machines, picking up punch boards and driving up to Chicago to buy bootleg beer from Al Capone's brewery, which he would bring back in Clyde's Packard. The only seat in the Packard was the drivers seat, so the rest of the car could be filled with kegs of beer or cartons of booze.

But Eddie and Clyde never really got along. Eddie had more of a sense of honor, where Clyde was devious. After a couple years Eddie talked Clyde into letting him open a restaurant on Knoxville at McClure called Eddie's Chop House. He ran that for several years but, eventually, the building was torn down and a new brick building was built. A new restaurant opened there called The Marine Room, owned by Bill Degaris and replacing Eddie's Chop House. After that Eddie and Mona Lucas bought a restaurant called Jennings on upper Main Street.

Clyde always felt bad that Lucas didn't like him, but around 1934, after liquor became legal again, Clyde talked Eddie into being his partner in a distributorship handling Hiram Walker and, later, other liquor labels. He named it G & L Distributors. The "G" was for Garrison and the "L" was for Lucas. But they eventually split up again because they just couldn't get along.

It was shortly after Clyde recovered from his wounds from the kidnap attempt that he got involved with the FBI, but this time it was on the right side of the law.

After the kidnapping and killing of Charles and Anne Morrow Lindberg's baby in 1932, Congress passed a law making kidnapping a Federal offense. It was right after that when Peoria's Dr. James W. Parker was kidnapped.

The FBI suspected the manager of the Hines Apartments on McClure Avenue was in on the Parker kidnapping. They came to Peoria and entered the case. The Feds brought along a group of Chicago's famed businessmen known as "The Secret Six," who were formed to combat gangland activities. One of the lead FBI guys was a crack shot named Buck Kempster. He had lost a couple fingers in an earlier gunfight but he was considered to be the FBI's best man with a machine-gun.

Since Clyde had also been a kidnap target and his wife was killed, the FBI contacted him figuring he would be sympathetic to catching the kidnappers of Dr. Parker. They were right!

Clyde's home was also on McClure, not far from the Hines Apartments and they rigged a phone in Clyde's house so that, every time the phone rang in the Hines manager's office, it also rang at Clyde's and they would listen in.

There were no tape recorders in those days so, when the phone conversation got interesting, they had a stenographer put on the headphones and take down the conversation in shorthand, so it could be used as evidence. As it turned out, Buck Kempster was the FBI man credited with getting the goods on the apartment manager that sent him to jail.

Dr. Parker was released after 18 days. It was later determined that Parker was held at a farm near Banner, Illinois. Eight of 11 people arrested in the plot, including an attorney and an ex-cop, went to the penitentiary with terms of from five to 25 years.

Buck Kempster lived in Clyde's house for about a month during this episode and the two became good friends. Buck also had a brother, Wilber, and a nephew, Harry, living in Peoria, so Buck quit the FBI and went to work for Clyde.

Clyde's wife, Cora was killed in 1930, and in the late 30s Clyde started going with Mary Howerton. They were engaged for 14 years. One day she said: "Clyde, I know enough about you to send you up to Joliet for the rest of your life so, it's time we got married." Clyde seemed to agree so . . . they got married!

John Lucas always liked "Uncle" Clyde because he was jovial and kind to the family. He said there were times during the Depression when Clyde would just come to the front door and hand John's mother 20 bucks. Needless to say, twenty dollars bought a lot of groceries during those lean Depression days.

About the time John went on to college, his parents divorced and in 1960, his dad went to California and developed a vending machine business. He eventually wound up in Las Vegas.

As mentioned earlier, for many years before the Sheltons came north to Peoria, Clyde Garrison controlled gambling in this area, both in town and the counties. He started with punch boards and hired people to get them into businesses. From there he went into slot machines. He was still active in the gambling racket even in the face of Carl Shelton's outfit, but never with them!

There was also another character in the 30s and 40s who had a reputation of being dangerous, although he never seemed to get too involved with the gangs. He was a former prize-fighter named Dwight "Snooks" Gordon. Snooks was a friend of Clyde Garrison, which automatically put him against the Sheltons.

Snooks usually hung out at The Mint, a saloon at 409 Fulton Street, which was one of the few successful holdouts from the Shelton gang. Maybe it was because of Snooks, who had a temper to compare with Bernie Shelton. The only difference was, Snook's temper was bad whether he was drunk *or* sober!

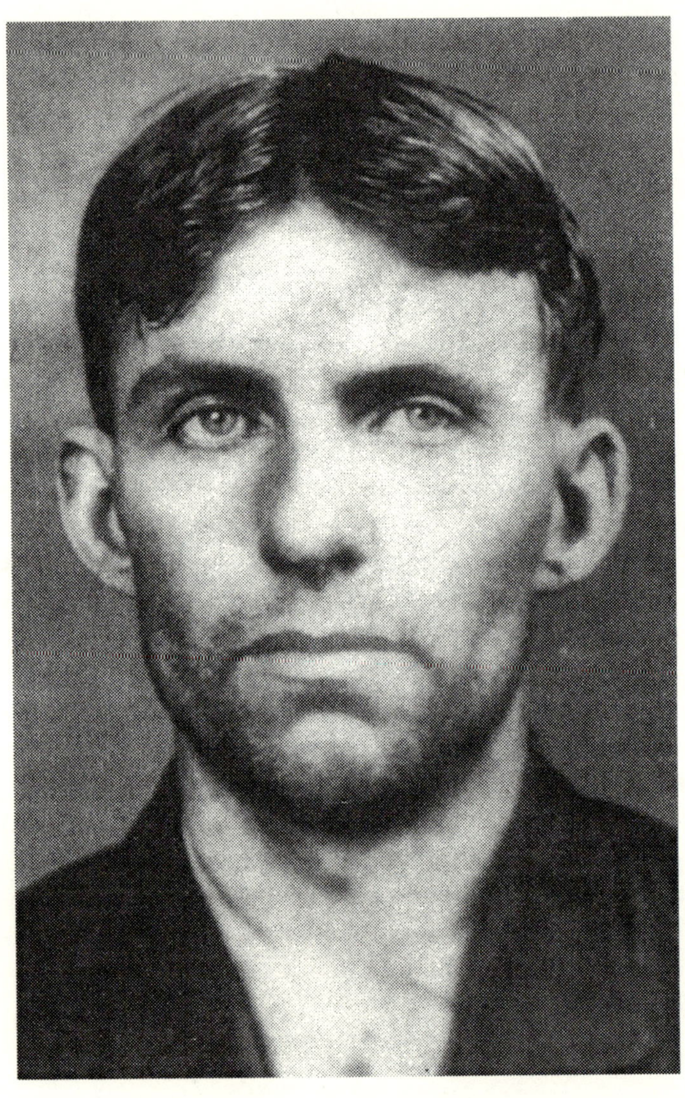

A young Carl Shelton as he appeared during the "Bloody Williamson County" days. (Photo from the Archives of the Peoria Journal Star.)

Roy Shelton, who was shot and killed while Driving his tractor in 1950. (Photo from the Archives of the Peoria Journal Star.)

A mean Bernie Shelton, especially when he was drinking.
(Photo from the Archives of the Peoria Journal Star.)

Southern Illinois bootlegger, Charlie Birger (center, sitting on the roof of the car) and his gang at their roadhouse, Shady Rest, in "Bloody Williamson County," in 1927. (A post card by G. Pruett of Herrin, I1.)

Charlie Birger, the man who headed the gang that fought the Sheltons in the bloody Williamson County war.
(From the book, "A Knight of Another Sort," by Gary DeNeal)

Art Newman
(From the book, "A Knight of Another Sort," by Gary DeNeal)

Al Hunt, the owner of Hunt's Drive-In, across the road from Bernie Shelton's Parkway tavern.
(Photo from the Archives of the Peoria Journal Star.)

Left to right: Carl Shelton talking to Ray Miller, operator of the Faust Club; Tony Couri who used his friendship with Carl to save the life of Joe Rafool; person behind Tony unidentified; and Genevieve Shelton, Bernie's wife. (Photo courtesy of Tony Couri.)

Standing from left: Al Stengle, a Joliet tavern and handbook owner and former partner of Clyde Garrison; Pearl Vaughn and Carl Shelton. Seated from left: Frank Kraemer; Sylvia, a friend of Buck Kempster; Mary Howerton, friend and future wife of Clyde Garrison; an unidentified woman; Harry Tyrell, silent partner of Carl Shelton; and Mrs. Dorothy Kraemer, wife of Frank Kraemer.
(Photo from the Archives of the Peoria Journal Star.)

Standing left to right: Young relative of Clyde Garrison; Buck Kempster; Frank Kraemer; Dorothy Kraemer, wife of Frank; Clyde Garrison; Betty Gordon, wife of "Snooks" Goordon. Seated left to right: Joe Jacobs; Tony Galento, championship boxer; and Dwight "Snooks" Gordon. Circa 1940. (Photo courtesy of John Lucas)

Standing left to right: Dwight "Snooks" Gordon; Richard Bradley; Claude U. Stone. Seated left to right: Clyde Garrison; Robert McCluggage, Clyde's partner in the Windsor Tap and brother to Mayor Dave McCluggage; Harry McBride, owner of the Palace Club; Jack Dempsey, championship boxer; and Dave McClugage, Mayor of Peoria. Circa 1940.
(Photo courtesy of John Lucas)

Carl O. Triebel became Peoria's "reform" mayor in 1945. He was also owner and operator of Ideal Troy Cleaners and Laundry.

Carl Shelton, the boss of the Shelton Gang that controlled gambling in Peoria until 1945.

(Photos from the archives of the Peoria Journal Star.)

The chairs on Bernie's porch where he and Gatewood talked while the recordings were being made of the supposed "shakedown" of a $25,000 bribe by Peoria State's Attorney Roy Hull. The microphone was hidden in the radio which was connected to the recorder in the kitchen on the other side of this window.

(Photo from the Archives of the Peoria Journal Star.)

The recorder in the kitchen of Bernie Shelton's home
that was used by Jack Ashby to record the conversation
between Bernie and Roy Gatewood on the porch
on the other side of the window.
(Photo from the Archives of the Peoria Journal Star.)

Jack Ashby, Bernie Shelton's partner in the Shelton
Amusement Company, testifying in Court.
(Photo from the Archives of the Peoria Journal Star.)

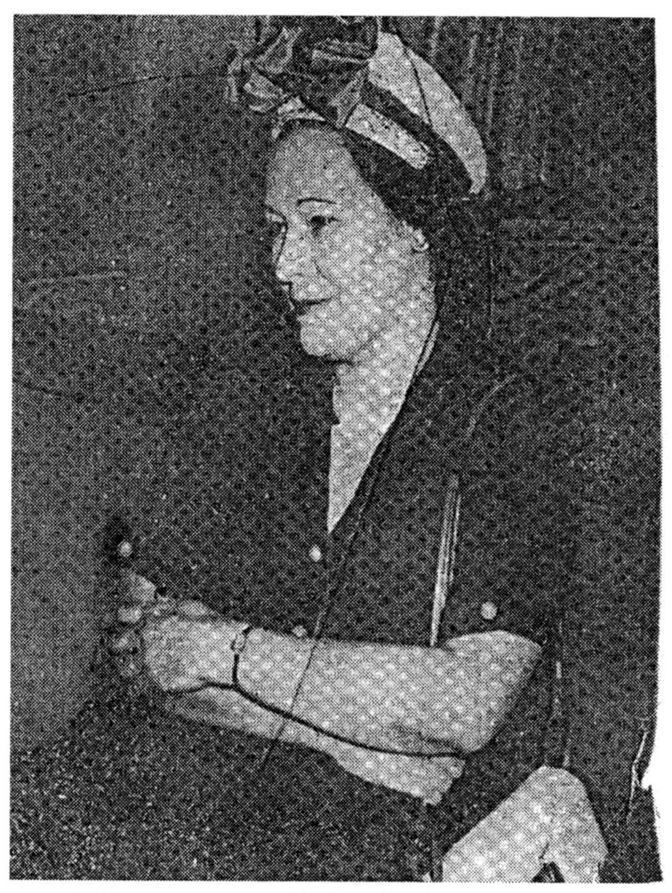

Mrs. Jack Ashby, who was present when, the Gatewood recording was made, waiting to testify before the Peoria grand jury. (Photo by a St. Louis Post-Dispatch photographer.)

Bernie Shelton was shot from the wooded hillside behind his Buick on the right just outside the Parkway Inn on Farmington Road in Peoria. He died a few minutes later at St. Francis Hospital.
(Photo from the Archives of the Peoria Journal Star.)

Sheriff Earl Spainhower (left) and Chief Deputy Sheriff Bill Littell, inspect the weapoin that killed Bernie Shelton. (Photo from the Archives of the Peoria Journal Star.)

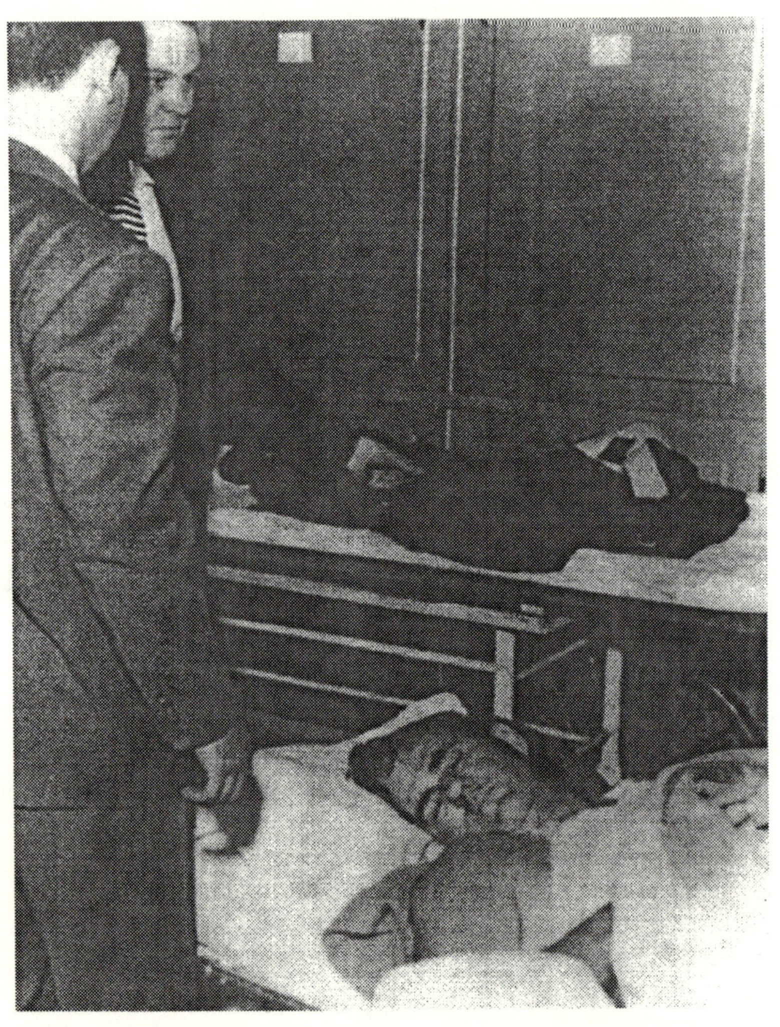

THE DEAD BODY OF BERNIE SHELTON
in the emergency room of St. Francis hospital, shortly after
he was shot on Farmington Road.
(Photo from the archives of the Peoria Journal Star.)

Family portrait of the Shelton Family that hung on the wall of Carl Shelton's home in Peoria. Standing left to right: Roy, Carl, Earl, Dalta and Bernie. Seated left to right: Lulu, their father and mother, and Hazel.

Chapter 12

More Gang Trouble But Carl Shelton Calls It Quits!

By 1945 trouble had begun to find the Sheltons again. Word had gone out from the Chicago syndicate that Carl and Bernie were each worth $10,000, dead or alive, and they didn't much care which way.

Five Chicago gunmen came to Peoria to try for the prize. It was believed that two Chicago hoods, with submachine guns, hid in the wooded bluff behind and above the Parkway Inn on Farmington Road, while the other three met with Carl and Bernie in the tavern but, during the conversation, Carl became suspicious and disappeared into the back room. He apparently made a quick phone call because, a short time later, two carloads of the Shelton gang arrived . . . and the gunmen went back to the "Windy City" with their tails between their legs.

Just recently a long-time Peorian, Jack Heintzman, reminisced about Bernie Shelton's murder. He recalled that, when he was just a youngster in the early 40's, one morning he and a group of kids including Bruce Saurs, Bob Dempsey, Tom Folkerts and Bill Brunner, who lived in West Peoria, were taking their usual shortcut through

St. Joseph's Cemetery on their way to play ball in lower Bradley Park, just across the road from the Parkway Inn. Their normal path was down from the end road in the cemetery through the wooded bluff behind the tavern, where they would emerge and walk across Farmington Road to the ball diamond.

Jack said, on this particular morning, just as they reached the bluff, a man came up out of the woods with a rifle in his hand. When Jack asked him what he was hunting, the man said, "I'm hunting rats!" With that, Jack said, the guy walked a short way up the cemetery's end road, where a car was waiting, and got in.

As Jack recalled, he was a short man of sleight build, dressed in a white shirt and dark trousers.

The question is, of course, could the "rats" he was hunting have been Carl and Bernie Shelton? He may well have been one of the Chicago hoods trying to cash in on the "dead or alive" reward.

Another problem for the Sheltons in 1945 was the election of Carl O. Triebel as Peoria's new mayor, replacing E. N. Woodruff. Triebel was also a Peoria businessman, who owned and operated Ideal Troy, a major Peoria cleaners and laundry. He had said later that he never ran as a reform candidate, but he did take it upon himself to clean up the town. (No pun intended.) One of the first things he did was to close down open gambling.

Triebel was the complete opposite of former mayor Woodruff. They were both members of old Peoria families, but Triebel believed that he was elected because the public was fed up with deteriorating public services such as poor garbage collection and potholes in the streets, as well as the previous administration's underworld connections.

Less than a month after he was elected mayor, Triebel learned that the vice lords and the politicians were both greedy, and that there is no such thing as "a little vice." It was said, "You couldn't spit in Peoria without asking Carl Shelton." A similar expression had also been said about the Shelton gang many years earlier down south.

The Sheltons controlled most of the gambling houses, slot machines and punch boards and Triebel indicated that many of Peoria's 20 aldermen were getting $200 to $500 a month from the slot machines that were in virtually every tavern, drug store and card shop in town.

Prostitution ran openly in three districts near Peoria's downtown. One on North Washington and another around South Jefferson and Walnut streets. A third, called "Prairie Alley," which ran from Franklin near South Adams Street to Aiken Street in what was known as the "South End" of town .

A "madam" named Pam Miller, who had a "house" in the 600 block of S. Jefferson, controlled most of it. On November 26, 1947, Bernie Shelton married another "madam," Genevieve Tabor, who had run a house next door to Pam's. All during this time, the police were protecting the houses and the streetwalkers.

Triebel claimed that, a few days before he took office, a Shelton representative named Ferdie McGrane paid him a call. Here's Triebel's account of the conversation as published in a national magazine article.

McGrane: "I've come about the slot machines."
Triebel: "What about them?"
McGrane: "We'll handle them for you."
Triebel: "You'll what?"
McGrane: "We'll take care of 'em. How much do you want out of 'em?"
Triebel: "Nothing."
McGrane: "All right; then we'll pay something into your campaign fund."
Triebel: "That won't be necessary."

McGrane: "Why not?"
Triebel: "Because there aren't going to be any slot machines."

Triebel said Ferdie's mouth flew open about a foot.

McGrane left and about five minutes later, the phone rang. It was Carl Shelton. He asked to come over and Triebel told him to come ahead.

Triebel described Carl as "a big, breezy chap, sort of a western businessman type." Here's Triebel's description of that conversation.

Shelton: "I hear you couldn't get together with McGrane."
Triebel: "That's right."
Shelton: "Did you mean what you said?"

Triebel nodded his head.

Shelton studied him for a minute, then smiled and said, "Well, I guess that'll give me more time to farm."

Shelton owned a big farm near Fairfield, Illinois and Triebel also had an interest in a couple farms so, according to Triebel, they talked about farming for the next half hour. Then they shook hands and Shelton left.

Triebel stated that was the last time he saw the "terrible" Carl Shelton.

Later, when Triebel was having trouble with some local hoodlums, Carl Shelton sent word to him that he'd take care of the situation if he wanted him to. But Triebel said, "Fortunately I was able to handle it myself, but it was comforting to know that Carl Shelton was not hostile toward me because I had pulled down his playhouse. Later, I learned that he liked and respected me for my position . . ."

Then, on the evening of February 20, 1946, Frank Kraemer, the owner of The Spot tavern on Knoxville hill and a partner with George Parks in the Par-K Club on Hamilton downtown, was reading a newspaper in his home's sunroom at 3900 Farmington Road, when a car pulled into the driveway.

A moment later there was a crash of glass and a bullet whistled over Frank's head. He yelled to his wife to take cover and, as he ran for the adjoining living room, five more shots rang out and three slugs were in his body. One shot hit his wristwatch, which stopped at 7:31 p.m.

A story had circulated that Carl Shelton found out Kraemr was seen talking to Carl's enemies in St. Louis shortly before this slaying happened.

On the following September 21st at 7:30 a.m. Joel (Joe) Nyberg's riddled and battered body was found on the Lacon Club golf course, a few miles north of Peoria. He was said to be one of, if not the most, indicted person in Peoria County history.

Whether this murder was connected with Frank Kraemer's or not, Nyberg was known to have been a friend of Frank. The question was, of course, could these murders have been connected to the Shelton gang? By now it was hard to tell who was on which side of Peoria's gang warfare without a scorecard, much like it had been in Southern Illinois.

Phil Stumpf, who was mentioned before as a part of the Penn-Julian gang in 1929, had by now jumped over from bootlegging to gambling after Prohibition, and met a death of withering gunfire just a month after Nyberg got his.

On the night of October 25th Stumpf and another man, Charles Logsdon, were at the Stork Club, on Big Hollow Road. They went there so Phil Stumpf could repair a slot machine.

Another car followed them back toward Peoria and riddled their car with bullets from a carbine rifle. A .38 caliber revolver, the type used to kill Joe Nyberg the month before, was found in the glove compartment of Stumpf's car.

Stumpf was killed outright with two slugs in him but Logsdon survived with just a minor injury.

Carl Shelton may have quit but gang warfare was still alive and well in Peoria!

And, although Carl told Mayor Triebel he was going to retire to the farm, he didn't leave town right away. First of all he had to tell his gang about his decision and tend to a few details before heading south to Fairfield.

Then on December 31, 1946, Carl and Pearl threw a New Year's Eve party at their Knoxville Avenue home. Pearl said the guest list included Mr.& Mrs. Harold Newsome. Harold had operated the Inglaterra Ballroom for 14 years, and Mrs. Newsome was a client of Pearl's in her beauty shop. She also said the list included Mr. & Mrs. Bill Manning; Bernie Shelton and Genevieve Tabor (before Bernie and Genevieve were married); Mr. & Mrs. Ray Walker; Mr. & Mrs. Glen Huntley, Pearl's relatives from Lindewood, Illinois; and Peoria County Sheriff Earl Spainhower. She also thought officers Lee Van Norman and Joe Materelli were there for awhile.

Newsome brought some hats and horns from the Inglaterra but didn't plan to stay long because Mrs. Newsome had to work the boxoffice at the ballroom later that night.

Spainhower later denied having been at the party or ever having any business transactions with the Sheltons.

A newspaper, however, had reported that the Sheltons raised $7,200 for his campaign fund but the sheriff said it wasn't true. He said he didn't seek or ask for support of any gambling syndicate during the election.

But Pearl claimed that, in May 1947, Spainhower went to the Kentucky Derby with Carl and her in her car, along with Renard McDermott, Carl's stepson, and Genelle Caudle. She said they stayed overnight at the Martin Tourist Rooms in Palmyra, Indiana, and they all went down to Louisville to the races the next day. She thought Carl had gotten all five tickets for the races and said Spainhower sat with them in their box.

Again, Spainhower denied he had gone to the Kentucky Derby with Carl and Pearl. He said he did go to the races but he saw them down there and just visited with them in their box.

Later, Spainhower admitted that he was at the same motel in Palmyra on the same night as the Sheltons but he claimed he was there with three men friends and didn't know the Sheltons were also there. He said he wouldn't name his men friends, for fear of bringing innocent people into it.

Chapter 13

Carl Died The Way He Lived . . .

But At The Wrong End of the Gun!

Carl Shelton apparently didn't need any more money and he had been spending more and more time on his farm near Fairfield. He was almost 60 years old now and he told his gang he intended to retire.

His mother still lived on the small farm on the Merriam Road near Fairfield, and his brother, Earl, farmed 900 acres on that same road. His oldest brother, Roy, also owned a farm in the area.

In addition to farming, Carl also owned a little gambling joint on the Fairfield court house square called The Farmer's Club and he was becoming fascinated with newly discovered oil wells in Wayne County. He brought his old friend Ray Walker back down from Peoria and began building a new home there. But Carl was soon to find that retiring from the rackets wasn't going to be automatic. He couldn't even stay out of trouble by living on his farm.

Most of the trouble was with the Harris-Vaughan clan, who lived in an area known as the Pond Creek bottoms. The Shelton, Harris and Vaughan families were distant relatives and they owned farms close together.

Charles "Black Charley" Harris grew up with Carl Shelton and had been associated with the gang when they were bootlegging back in East St. Louis. In 1927 he was sent to prison. He was paroled early, but he violated his parole in 1932 and was sent back until he finished his term in 1937. There are several stories as to why Harris went to prison.

One story was that Harris was caught with his own counterfeit money. Another was that he went to prison by taking the rap for the Sheltons because it was the gang's bogus bills and he refused to squeal, thus taking the blame in true gangland fashion.

Black Charley said that, after he was released from prison, instead of the Shelton's welcoming him back into the fold, they shunned him. Enraged by this, he went back to the Pond Creek bottoms area and nursed his grudge.

The feud apparently first festered when Carl did offer to help Harris purchase a farm and rehabilitate himself after his jail term, but Charley said Carl later changed his mind and decided to keep the farm for himself.

Carl had obtained a mortgage on it after an affray in 1940 when Harris shot and killed an oil field worker named "Blackie" Anderson, after Anderson had stabbed him. The shooting took place at a roller skating rink on the outskirts of Fairfield, which was operated in a partnership between Harris and a sister of Carl's. During this skirmish, a stray bullet struck Carl, who was a bystander, but the bullet was deflected by an eyeglass case in his pocket.

Harris was released on a $10,000 bond, furnished by Carl, and a grand jury later found the shooting constituted justifiable homicide.

It was about this time that Harris was telling friends that Carl had assumed a mortgage on the farm but he, Harris, had raised enough money to pay it off.

Later, in the fall of 1947, after Carl moved back to his farm, the Sheltons and the Harris-Vaughan clan quarreled over some cattle. Charley had accused "Big" Earl of turning out cattle on Harris' grazing land and Earl countered with a charge that Harris was rustling his stock. A fight ensued and two of Charley's friends, Virgil Vaughan and Johnny Moore, were pistol-whipped by young members of the Shelton mob, reputedly including Dellos Wylie. A short time later the feud reached its climax.

About 8 a.m. on the morning of October 23, 1947, Carl was driving his Jeep on a country road near his farm. He was on his way to get a load of soybeans and following him in his truck were Ray Walker and Carl's 28-year-old nephew, "Little" Earl Shelton.

"Little" Earl later said that, earlier, they had heard a honking of horns in the hills. "It sounded like it might be signals," he recalled. The day was a hot and dusty one. They had topped a rise above a little creek and as they headed down, "Little" Earl and Walker saw a black car in a lane behind some underbrush just past a bridge. As Carl's Jeep neared the bridge, gunfire came from the underbrush.

Carl's Jeep swerved and he fell out of it. "Little" Earl and Ray jumped from their truck and dived into the ditch, a short way behind Carl. Walker later testified that "Little" Earl, "hollered for Carl to get down with us, but he didn't seem to hear. Carl said . . . 'Well, Charley, it's me, Carl . . . you know me. Charley, you've killed me, don't shoot no more, you've done killed me.'"

They said that in a moment the car in the lane drove off. Earl asked Ray if he thought it was safe to try to escape. Walker answered he didn't know, but they couldn't stay there all day, so they got back in the truck and drove to town. First they telephoned Bernie in Peoria.

Then they picked up "Big" Earl and a state policeman and drove back to the shooting scene.

Carl's body lay in an elderberry thicket in the ditch. He was dead. His cap was found 20 feet away. He was riddled with rifle, pistol and machinegun bullets. The policeman wanted to leave his body undisturbed until they could photograph it but "Big" Earl said, "Boys, I hate to see him in that position; let's lift him up on the road." When they lifted his body, they found his revolver beneath him. It had been fired five times.

A 68-year-old farmer, Henry F. Wagner, whose home was at the head of a lane 200 yards from where the shooting took place, told a reporter that he was looking at a clover field on his brother's farm across from his, when the Shelton's drove by. He said, "Carl was in front in a jeep, and Ray and 'Little' Earl were following in a truck. They all waved and called good morning.

"All of a sudden I heard two shots. Within a few seconds there was a regular burst of shots. I couldn't tell whether it was a machine-gun but it was awful fast shooting. There were at least 40 shots and they sounded different, as though a lot of people were shooting."

The farmer later saw Carl's body by the side of the road as he went to the mailbox. When the authorities arrived from Fairfield the sheriff found a hubcap from a Ford car and a quantity of empty shells, most of which were of a foreign make. The hubcap had apparently been shot off of the car by Carl.

The next day "Big" Earl viewed Carl's body at the Fairfield undertaking parlor. It contained 16 bullet wounds.

Shelton's 85-year-old mother said, "Carl led a good life, despite his troubles years ago." Pearl, Carl's new wife from Peoria (although they had lived together for years) tearfully said, "I'm just bewildered."

"Little" Earl later testified that he saw Charley Harris

firing a gun and Walker said he saw an armed stranger attired like a city dweller in a suit, hat and dress shirt.

Sheriff Bradshaw told a *St. Louis Post-Dispatch* reporter that "Little" Earl related that, as he and Walker fled, they saw Harris, armed with a rifle, guarding an entrance to the road and later saw him assisting one of his companions into the back seat of a black Ford sedan used by the slayers. The companion had apparently been wounded when Carl returned their fire.

Carl Shelton's funeral was the largest ever seen in Fairfield, and even his good friend, Tony Couri, drove down from Peoria with Ferd McGrane the day before. First, they went to the homestead farm and gave condolences to Carl's mother, who thanked him for being Carl's friend and getting her soap powder during the war. She also insisted they stay overnight at the house but they didn't want to inconvenience her and decided to go to a hotel in town.

There was a lot of talk of the trouble over Carl's death and more than 1,500 curious people overflowed the First Methodist Episcopal Church to witness the last rites. The first 800 people got seats but several hundred more stood in a drizzling rain on the sidewalk across the street. More than 80 cars lined the four-mile route taken by the funeral cortege from the old Shelton homestead and, later, to the cemetery. Dozens of police directed traffic, including seven Illinois state troopers.

Fearing that Carl's relatives and friends, some of whom were seen wearing shoulder holsters, might seek revenge, E. L. Curneal, elder of the Primitive Baptist Church preached the sermon, "Vengeance is mine, saith the Lord. Nothing is solved by vengeance and wrath—only vengeance and wrath will follow."

Following the services by Dr. C. L. Peterson, pastor of the First Methodist Episcopal Church, more than 1,500 people filed past Carl's bronze casket for a last look at the slain man. Some of the flowers were tagged, "Our Pal."

Carl was buried beside his father, Ben Shelton, in the family plot in Maple Hill Cemetery.

Elder Curneal turned out to be a pretty good prophet because "Vengeance and wrath" certainly *did* follow!

Chapter 14

Did "Black Charley" Really Kill Carl Shelton?

The *St. Louis Post-Dispatch* said it had received reports that four gangsters from St. Louis and East St. Louis had been visiting one of two gambling casinos on the East Side of St. Louis every morning for a month before Carl's murder in October 1947. They would place their pistols and shotguns on a table in front of them and discuss the search for Shelton. It was also stated that, shortly before the murder, a stranger, whose description answered that of "Black Charley" Harris, was with the group.

St. Louis police questioned David "Chippy" Robinson and another former Egan gang member, Steve Ryan. These two were reported to be associated in a cigar store vending machine company. Three other men were being sought. They were Louis "Red" Smith, an Egan gangster; Elmer Dowling, a St. Louis hoodlum and Frank "Buster" Wortman, an East Side gangster.

Wayne County State's Attorney, Virgil W. Mills, also announced that he would ask the FBI at Springfield, Illinois to enter the case because Harris had fled across state lines, a violation of the federal fugitive flight law.

Mills also told the *Post Dispatch* that witnesses said they saw a black Ford club coupe, with four men in it, two miles south of the shooting scene shortly after Shelton was killed on October 23.

Someone described the driver as a "very large man with huge shoulders, who seemed to dwarf the other passengers." Their description of another occupant answered to that of a notorious St. Louis gangster.

Mills also said another witness told of seeing this same car on Pond Creek Road, three weeks before the murder. Illinois State Highway Police theorized that, if this witness was correct about the earlier sighting, it may have been an aborted attempt to get Shelton then, but Carl had been called to Peoria on business about some oil land leases and didn't return home for a week.

What no one knew at the time was that Carl had also gone to Madisonville, Kentucky with his Peoria live-in girl friend, Pearl Vaughan, to get married on October 13, just *ten days before* his assassination. Pearl was a member of the Vaughan clan from the same Pond Creek bottoms area as Carl and "Black Charley" Harris.

When the coroner's inquest into Carl Shelton's death was held, the jury's verdict was that Shelton was slain by "persons unknown," but they recommended that Harris be held for further investigation.

The most damaging testimony against Harris was that of Ray Walker and "Little" Earl Shelton. They were with Carl when he was killed and testified they saw Harris running from the scene with a gun in his hand. Young Shelton also said he saw Harris fire one shot. But the testimony of a Mrs. Gladstone Keen tended to dispute this. She told the jury she saw Harris pass her home, three-quarters of a mile north of the shooting, about the same time the shots were fired.

In his testimony Ray Walker recalled that, at the scene of Carl's murder, as he crouched beneath a bridge to escape the gunfire, he heard a terse conversation between two unidentified assailants. Ray testified that one said, "Let's finish them," and his companion replied, "They are finished, let's get going." He said they then heard the sound of a car rattling over several wooden bridges along a country road south of the shooting.

In the meantime Charley Harris and his 20-year-old niece, Beatrice (Jakie) Suddarth Bell, who was apparently with him in his car when he was supposedly seen by "Little" Earl and Walker in the area where Carl was killed, suddenly disappeared. They were subsequently arrested in Tulsa, Oklahoma on October 30 at the All American Bus Depot. Harris seemed visibly shaken when arrested but he later signed extradition papers to be returned to Fairfield.

They had purchased two bus tickets to Phoenix, Arizona. The niece said she was en-route to a sister's home there where she planned to enter a nursing school. She told the press that her legal name was Beatrice Suddarth but she had adopted the Bell name because it was her mother's first husband's name and she had been reared with the Bell children.

The grand jury later convened on November 12. Fourteen men and nine women were impaneled at Fairfield by Circuit Judge, Benjamin W. Evoaldi. In the next two days witnesses in the Shelton case were heard, including "Little" Earl Shelton, Ray Walker, and (Jakie) Suddarth, who was a surprise witness.

Local residents were unaware of her presence in Fairfield. After she was released in Tulsa, she had presumably continued on to the home of a sister in Tucson, Arizona and brought back from there to testify.

She appeared frightened as the sheriff escorted her from the residential section of the county jail to the jury room. She kept the sheriff between her and a group of Sheltons in the hall. This group included Roy, "Big" Earl and "Little" Earl Shelton, along with Ray Walker.

"Big" Earl later remarked to a *Post-Dispatch* reporter, "I don't see why they guard those people. It was my brother who was killed, I should be protected."

Miss Suddarth then spent 13 minutes before the jury. She testified that she and Harris were driving to Charley's farm and reached the ambush scene shortly after Carl Shelton was killed.

Friends of the Sheltons believed that their old nemesis, Charley Harris, had fingered Carl and that Carl was killed by East St. Louis gunmen employed by the Chicago syndicate.

At the end of the grand jury hearings on Friday, November 15, Charles Harris was exonerated when the Wayne County Grand Jury concluded its investigation by returning a "no true bill." A newspaper reporter was the first to tell "Big" Earl that the jury had cleared Harris. Earl's face was impassive as he nodded his head. He then quietly left the courtroom.

So, with the grand jury's refusal to indict Harris, Carl Shelton's murder remains unsolved to this day.

Carl Shelton died without a will. Ironically, he had made an appointment to discuss one with Frank Borah, an accountant and former business associate, the day he was killed. Borah was later named co-administrator of Carl's estate, along with Carl's wife of ten days, Pearl Vaughan Shelton.

Borah believed Carl held considerable real estate in the names of "straw parties," and a search would be made for real estate in Fairfield, Peoria, Flora, East St. Louis and also in Madison County.

The Marriage Bond certificate stated that Carl and Pearl were married by Rev. C. R. Mathews and the witnesses were Jess McGary and Sarah L. McGary. Carl Shelton stated he was born in Chicago and resided in Henderson Kentucky, Route #3 and was 50 years old. Pearl stated she was born in White County, Illinois, the daughter of Cleve and Ida Abshere Vaughan, resided in Jacksonville, Florida and was 35 years old. These addresses, of course, were not true. Carl also listed his occupation as "Oil Business" and he was actually 59, not 50.

So now, instead of the family realizing Carl's estate, it would be shared with his widow of ten days. This so infuriated Bernie, who owned the Shelton Amusement Company in Peoria, in partnership with Carl, that he visited Pearl one night at her Knoxville Avenue home and, with a gun in her back, forced her to sign over Carl's half-interest in the juke box business. At this point, Pearl decided she had better get an attorney . . . ***and fast!***

After Bernie's visit Pearl became very frightened. It also appears that she had been playing a pretty dangerous game of her own, because the man who brought her to a Peoria attorney's office to seek legal counsel, was a secret lover she had been seeing while she was living with Carl Shelton.

The attorney agreed to represent her and, later, he also gave her some personal advice that may have saved her life, as we will see later.

Carl Shelton's death was investigated by the State of Illinois but it was stalemated following the failure of the Wayne County grand jury to return any indictments, and authorities were fearful of an all-out gang war over gambling rights in Illinois.

They noted that the dice games of Dee Jones, an East Alton gambler and associate of Carl Shelton, were shut down a week before Carl was killed, while a rival Hyde Park gambling casino at Venice, Illinois was running full blast. The Hyde Park Club had been taken over by former members of the old Egan gang and representatives of the Chicago gambling syndicate.

Also, the week before the killing, an East Side man told the St. Louis police that he had stopped in at the

Plantation Inn Tavern near Fairmount City and observed four men talking to the waitress and a bartender. One of the men, he said, offered to bet the bartender a roll of bills that they would get Shelton within a few weeks.

The Sheltons controlled gambling through a central strip of Illinois south of Peoria and extending into parts of Indiana and Kentucky. The ornate Colony Club near Cairo was a juicy plumb, with customers from Illinois, Missouri and Kentucky. This club was operated by Joe Dodds, a former Herrin nightclub owner, and had run without interruption through World War II. It was now considered in the expansion plans of the syndicate.

A third gang at Herrin was also slowly gaining strength under the leadership of Roy "Tony" Armes, an ex-convict and brother of "Blackie" Armes, a former inmate at Alcatraz with "Buster" Wortman. Tony Armes and another brother "Lefty", also an ex-convict, had recently joined forces with Wortman and the syndicate. It was said that overtures had been made to "protect" the Colony Club and eliminate Shelton's interest in it.

Also, during the past year Harry Stearns, a black man, who was also Carl Shelton's East St. Louis representative, had been chased out of East St. Louis. When he left, the interest he held for the Sheltons in several small games, was taken over by Wortman and his group.

Then in May, George Williams, a Shelton associate and Havana, Illinois tavern owner, narrowly escaped death when his car was riddled with 23 bullets. He crawled out of the car unscathed but abandoned his tavern venture, which was said to be financed by the Sheltons.

Chapter 15

Now It's Bernie' Turn For Big Trouble, And More!

When Bernie got back to Peoria from Carl's funeral he was furious to find that Harry Tyrrell had already taken over the gambling business there. He seemed obsessed with the idea that he, Carl's brother, should take over, but apparently Peoria's gambling proprietors had already decided that Tyrrell should have control. They felt that Bernie would be too explosive a person to handle the business end of things and Harry would make a good business manager for everyone concerned.

Pete Petrakos didn't know Bernie Shelton until after Carl was killed, when Bernie called him and said he'd like to meet him at the Parkway office. Pete expressed sympathy about Carl's death. Bernie told him he was going to be a good boy now. He was going to stop drinking and run things in Peoria. But what Bernie needed now was a contact with Claude Stone, publisher of the *Peoria Star*. Bernie indicated he knew Carl had Stone on his payroll.

A city detective had said Claude parked his car around the corner of Carl's house at night once a month and visited with him. Bernie asked Pete to make the same connection for him.

Pete contacted Stone who allegedly told him to take him to the Parkway office the next day. It was January 1948. The two met privately and afterwards, according to Petrakos, Stone told him he thought they could get along all right. A month later Bernie asked Pete to bring Stone down again. This time Pete said the three of them sat in the car and Bernie commented that they had a fine arrangement and there would be no more "sensation" in the county. Pete also said Bernie threw some money at the judge, who counted it and asked about the *Peoria Journal*. He said Bernie told him not to worry, they'd take care of them.

Pete said Stone felt, now that Bernie had stopped drinking, he'd be as fine an operator as Carl but Petrakos was afraid. He had read what the Sheltons did years ago in southern Illinois and he felt Bernie was still a bad one. He also knew Bernie had kicked a man and beat him up.

The rumor was that it was Tom Murphy, then chairman of the Peoria County Board of supervisor, who had been beaten to a pulp in front of then sheriff, Swords, and a couple of other witnesses in the lobby of the Pere Marquette Hotel. Sheriff Swords owned the Pere Marquette and the story that was being spread around town by some of his enemies was that he had purchased the hotel with the money he made by cooperating with the gamblers.

Pete said, about a month after their meeting with Bernie, Shelton called him in and gave him an envelope for Stone and continued to do so every month. Pete got curious one month and carefully opened the envelope. He said it had $600 in $50 bills in it.

For all intents and purposes, gambling had slowed down, if not shut down, in the city under Mayor Triebel but it was continuing sporadically in the county areas.

Jack Ashby said Carl had been doing business with Charlie Somogyi, the chief investigator of the Peoria State's Attorney's office under Roy Hull and he also knew

Carl had been doing business with Peoria County Sheriff, Earl Spainhower, who took office on December 1, 1946.

After Carl's death an arrangement had allegedly been made between Tyrrell and Bernie that Bernie would pick up the monthly payoff envelopes at Tyrrell's car dealership for Somogyi of the State's Attorney's office; Roscoe Zerwekh, chairman of the Peoria County Board of Supervisors; and Pete Petrakos, for Judge Stone of the *Peoria Star*. These envelopes would be picked up at the amusement company, while Spainhower, who had previously gotten his at Carl's house, would now pick his up at Tyrrell's Studebaker company, where he got his car serviced monthly.

Ashby said it irked Bernie that every month, after the envelopes were distributed, Somogyi would call and say the "boss" was unhappy with the amount.

Roy Hull had run for office for a second term in the primary election in the spring of 1948 but lost the election. It was rumored that he blamed the Sheltons and the gambling syndicate in general and there was talk he'd love to "get" Bernie Shelton before he left office. If this was true, his opportunity came on the evening of Sunday, May 30, 1948, when a fight broke out in the Parkway Inn.

Bernie and Ray Walker had been to a horse show that day in Macon, Illinois. After they got back Bernie picked up his wife and they, along with Walker, went to the "Parkway" to eat. They were met there by Jack and Mary Ashby and, a little later, more friends joined them; Mr.& Mrs. Hoblitzel and Mr.& Mrs. John Kelly.

Bernie was in a bad mood because his horse didn't take first place at the show and he was drinking beer, which he usually didn't do these days.

A man named Stanley, a radical character they called "The Old Communist," came in and sat down next to Bernie, which was a mistake, because of Bernie's penchant for getting mean when he drank.

Stanley started making profane remarks about women who came into a tavern like this, and Bernie slapped him in the face. The old man ran out the back door with Bernie, Walker and Ashby running after him. A Navy veteran named Dick Murphy, Jr., who had been playing cards in the tavern, came out to see what happened.

They didn't catch the old man so Shelton, Ashby and Walker went next door to the Mecca Supper Club bar and had another drink, where Walker became very sick. He had been out in the hot sun all day at the horse show without much to eat. He suggested to Bernie that he'd better go home. Ashby offered to drive him in his car, and went back into the Parkway to tell his wife he'd be right back. Clarence Donovan, the Parkway proprietor had also gone outside. He came back in and told Ashby he'd better get out there quick because Walker was in trouble.

According to onlookers, two men were holding Walker by both arms while Murphy was hitting him. Ray's shirt was torn and he was bleeding down the front. Ashby broke it up and he and Bernie walked Walker back over near the Parkway building. At this point, Al Hunt was seen coming across the road from his drive-in with a pistol in his hand.

Ashby hurriedly put Walker in his car and sped away to get Ray out of there and drive him home. But Jack began worrying about Bernie back at the tavern where Al Hunt was brandishing a gun. Walker was feeling better by now so, instead of driving Ray all the way home, Jack dropped him off on Jefferson street and drove back to the tavern to see about Bernie.

When he got back, there were two policemen on the scene and a large crowd milling around. Someone said they had taken some people to jail and, as it turned out, Bernie was one of them. Someone in the crowd said

Bernie had turned Al Hunt around, and with a pistol now in Hunt's back, walked him back across the road, suggesting that he mind his own business.

The police had taken Bernie and Kelly down to the county jail first, and brought Al Hunt in later. The Sheriff indicated they were going to hold Bernie overnight and Murphy and Hunt were going to sign warrants against them. Bernie wasn't released until the next day but, before it was over, three charges were filed against Bernie; three against Walker and three against Kelly.

Jack Ashby said that, some time later, Roy Gatewood, who was a good friend of States Attorney Hull, drove his car up to the Shelton Amusement Company and Bernie got in and talked with him. When Bernie came back into the office he told Ashby that Gatewood said Hull was prepared to throw Bernie's case out of court for $25,000. Bernie was livid and said he wouldn't pay that much . . . that he'd go to jail first.

After hearing this, Ashby got an idea. He asked Bernie if he thought he could get Gatewood to repeat that offer to him. If so, he'd like to get a recording of the conversation without Gatewood's knowledge. Bernie thought it was a great idea and told him to set it up.

Jack went down to Klaus Radio store on Main Street and bought a slightly used professional record-maker with all the equipment necessary and took it back to the company office. He tested it with Bernie and a couple friends, who didn't know what it was going to be used for.

The next evening, Sunday, June 27, Ashby took the equipment out to the Shelton farm where he, Bernie and their two wives sat it up. Ashby took an old table model radio of Bernie's and sat it on a table on the sun porch. He wired it up with a microphone inside the radio's speaker and ran a cable through a window between the porch and the kitchen. He hooked it up to the record-machine that had been set up on the kitchen table.

Then they rearranged the furniture on the porch. There were three seats out there, so Mrs. Shelton placed a heavy sewing machine in one, leaving only two seats: one on either side of the "radio."

Jack tested the headsets and found they were very sensitive to other surrounding noises, so they removed a canary in its cage, disconnected the refrigerator and wrapped the phone in blankets to muffle any ring.

Now the trick would be to get Gatewood to come in on the porch to talk. He might be reluctant to come in because he had been afraid of Bernie ever since Bernie had pistol-whipped him in the Sportsman's Club. He'd never talk to Bernie after that unless it was inside his car or out in the open.

At this point Bernie called Gatewood on the phone. He asked him to come out to the farm and talk, indicating interest in Hull's offer. Roy said he couldn't come because his wife had the car that night.

Thinking that the deal was off for the night, the two couples put all the furniture back in place, when the phone rang again. It was Gatewod saying his wife had come home with the car and he'd be right out.

Gatewood only lived a couple miles down the road and they scrambled to get everything back in place. The women took off their shoes and joined Jack in the kitchen where he sat with the headphones on and started the machine.

As an excuse to get Roy on the porch, Bernie quickly took off his trousers, shoes and socks and sat rubbing his feet as Gatewood drove up.

Roy wanted Bernie to come out to talk in the car but Bernie said he couldn't because his arthritis was acting up and he asked Roy to come in on the porch where it was cool. Roy hesitated and then came in.

Bernie was sitting on one side of the radio, which only left Roy the seat on the other side of it. Now the two could only speak across the "radio" and Gatewood was unknowingly being recorded.

The entire conversation was recorded, including the profanity they used, which was edited out of what later appeared in the newspapers. It was first printed in the *St. Louis Post-Dispatch* on August 6, 1948 and repeated in the *Peoria Star* on August 10th.

Here are some of the highlights of the four records made of the conversation:

Shelton: "Oh, come in, Roy."

Gatewood: "You got a sweet place out here."

Shelton: "Huh? Yeah. Cool ain't it?"

Gatewood: "Yes."

Shelton: "I have been thinking about that twenty-five thousand. Do you suppose he made a mistake?"

Gatewood: "No."

Shelton: "You know, I have the darndest time with your name. It's a 'hardy.' G-a-t . . ."

Gatewood: "e-w-o-o-d. Gatewood."

Shelton: "How do you think, Roy? How do you think he could mess this case around?"

Gatewood: "I don't know, Bernie, but he's not going to mess you around."

Shelton: "He said he would throw all those indictments out but one, some way."

Gatewood: "He was going to put them all out but one indictment, see, and that's all, and that is to carry the . . . It's to make the jury, the grand jury . . . so the grand jury won't come back to him, and then he is going to throw the whole—damned thing out in September."

Shelton: "I just got to thinking about that twenty-five thousand, see, and I said, 'Well, I'm going to call Roy up and just see.'"

Gatewood:	"I don't blame you for thinking about it."
Shelton:	"But I tell you I just made up my mind I ain't giving him a penny because he's trying to frame me."
Gatewood:	"I know he's trying to frame you . . . Well, I think the indictment comes up Monday."
Shelton:	"Yeah."
Gatewood:	"Now listen, I want to tell you something. If you don't do this, stay hid out. Now, do that because they are going to get you down at that jail."
Shelton:	"Yeah?"
Gatewood:	"They're going to get you down there at jail and make you sweat, see, in there for a week, anyway, because they won't accept anybody's bond, see . . ."
Gatewood:	"Well, call me any—damned time you want anything."
Shelton:	"Yeah, O.K., Roy."
Gatewood:	"I'm not too—damned busy so I can't do a man A favor."
Shelton:	"No, but I just got to thinking about that twenty-five and it got to worrying me, and I thought "Well –, 'You know, if you was guilty of anything, it would be different, for'—sake."
Gatewood:	"And he's going to get it from any—damned angle he can. That's the reason he left on his—damned vacation. He got to thinking about it after he went up there, he got to thinking about it. He left his kids up there."
Shelton:	"Minnesota, huh?"
Gatewood:	"Yeah."

State's Attorney Hull later denied the bribery charge and said his life had been threatened.

At first Bernie didn't want anyone but his wife and the Ashby's to know about the recordings until he could talk to a lawyer. But a day later he decided to let Judge Stone of the *Peoria Star* hear them and he told Petrakos to set up a meeting for the weekend of July 4, which Pete did.

Then Bernie suddenly called off the meeting because he heard there was going to be a horse sale at Muscatine, Iowa that weekend and he wanted to sell one of his Palomino stallions. So Petrakos cancelled the meeting with Stone. (Stone didn't hear the records until July 24th.)

But Pete seemed very inquisitive about the trip. Thinking it was a horse show, he told Bernie he'd like to go along, but when he was told it was just a horse sale, he lost interest but still curious about where the sale was going to be. Bernie finally told him it was going to be at Muscatine, Iowa.

Then he asked Bernie if he was going by way of Galesburg and, if so, he said he could recommend a good place there to stop and eat.

On Friday, July 2, Bernie and Genevieve, along with Mr. & Mrs. Doc Williams, left by car for Muscatine with Doc Williams driving. The horse was sent by a separate truck and horse trailer.

That same afternoon a strange phone call came to the Ashby's house. Jack was repairing a machine at the Toonerville Trolley tavern on Farmington Road, when his wife, Mary, called him saying that Ray Walker had just called from Fairfield, asking if Bernie had been shot and was in St, Francis Hospital? There was a rumor down there that Bernie had been ambushed in Peoria. Jack went home and checked out everything he could but the story turned out to be untrue, although the rumor had been broadcast over a radio station down south.

As it turned out, Bernie had made it to Muscatine but only stayed overnight. He and his wife and friends had returned the following day.

The next evening Ray Walker and John Kelly came up to Bernie's farm. They had been hiding out in Fairfield but had to appear in court in Peoria the following

Tuesday anyway, so they came up early to check on Bernie.

That night Bernie, Walker and Kelly, along with some other friends, went to the Parkway. Johnny Robinson was there and he wanted to see Bernie. He had a message for him from a girl Robinson used to go with. She said Carl Shelton had been a good friend to her in the past and had loaned her $200 when she needed it. Now she wanted to return the favor to Carl's brother.

She had told Robinson to tell Bernie that he was supposed to have gotten killed the past Thursday while going to Ashby's house. If he wasn't killed then, he was to get it on the way to Muscatine the next day.

This news came as a big surprise to Bernie because there were only three people who were supposed to know about the Iowa trip; Ray Walker, Jack Ashby and . . . PETE PETRAKOS!

The next day Robinson told Ashby that the lady had also told him that Buster Wortman and his St. Louis gang were coming to Peoria in two Mercury automobiles. Ashby asked Johnny for the lady's name but he wouldn't tell him. Then Jack asked if Johnny could get her to talk to Bernie personally. He indicated that he'd try but she was married to a man at Caterpillar and they were out of town on vacation. He said he'd get in touch with her when she got back.

It was obvious to Bernie that somebody had leaked the information of his trip to Iowa . . . and now, one of the only three who were supposed to know, Pete Petrakos, had suddenly, and mysteriously, left town.

It was always disgusting to Ashby how overly friendly Petrakos acted with Bernie. How he would put his arms around him and pat him on the back saying, "I love that man." It was making Jack wonder if this could be the same man who was trying to put the finger on

Bernie. Could Pete be spying for someone regarding Bernie's comings and goings?

The night after the recordings were made Ted Link, a reporter with the *St. Louis Post-Dispatch*, came to Peoria to cover the story. He had been on vacation and the newspaper had assigned a reporter named Harris to cover the story in Peoria until he got back. But when the story broke about the recordings the paper called Link back from vacation and assigned him to Peoria because he had known the Sheltons for many years. Jack Ashby, Genevieve Shelton and Ray Walker informed him about the records.

About four weeks later, on the morning of Monday, July 26, 1948, Bernie left his Golden Rule farm and drove down to the Parkway. After tending to some business, he asked Alex Ronitis, one of the bartenders, to follow him in his car to a Peoria Buick auto agency, where he planned to leave his Buick sedan to be serviced.

He and Ronitis started to the door together but Alex had left a pack of cigarettes on the bar and went back to get them while Bernie walked on out to his car alone. As he got to the car, which was parked on the west side of the building, a shot rang out and Bernie fell across the front of his car. He rose slowly and staggered back into the bar and sat down. He told Ronitis and another bartender, Edward O'Connor, "They got me in the woods." O'Connor immediately phoned for an ambulance.

Al Hunt at his Drive-In across the road again became involved in an action involving Bernie Shelton. He told reporters he was sitting in his office and heard the shot ring out. Glancing out the window, he saw Shelton slump across his car and he immediately called the sheriff's office.

Bernie insisted on walking to the ambulance when it arrived, but then consented to lay down on a stretcher and the ambulance headed for St. Francis hospital. Earl Stevens, the ambulance attendant, said Shelton became excited on seeing a green Chevrolet behind the ambulance and called out, "Watch that green car." The ambulance speeded up and got Bernie to the hospital, where he died at 11:46 a.m.

Chief Deputy Sheriff Bill Littell and other county deputies later searched the woods at the scene of the murder and found a .351 Winchester rifle about 300 feet up the slope. A discharged cartridge was found about 110 feet up from where Shelton was hit. Deputy's later also searched the tavern parking lot and found a soft-nosed slug, similar to the bullets found in the rifle.

From information gathered, the deputies believed the killer was driven by a companion to St. Joseph's Cemetery at the top of the slope above the tavern in a dark, possibly green, Chevrolet.

Two cemetery workmen, Barnard Klaas and Thomas Mitchell, saw the speeding car as it entered the cemetery gate, thought later to be on the way to drop off the rifleman. They said the occupants were well-dressed men and the car was driven to the back area of the cemetery, just above the tavern.

They didn't see the car leave but it was deduced that it waited to pick up the killer and it was believed it might have been the car that later followed the ambulance. A later check, however, ruled out this theory.

The next night Pete Petrakos suddenly returned from his trip out of town, as mysteriously as he left. Interestingly he had left on July 3, the day ***after*** the rumor that Bernie had earlier been killed. And just as interestingly, he returned around midnight on July 27, the night ***after*** Bernie was actually gunned down. Could this possibly be just coincidence?

And now, something else seemed peculiar. Now that Bernie really had been murdered, Petrakos, the man who said how much he "loved this man," didn't even call Bernie's wife when he returned. He didn't send flowers, he didn't contact any of Bernie's friends and of course, he didn't attend funerals, **not even Bernie's, the man he said he loved so much!**

Another unusual development occurred. Sheriff Earl Spaihower happened to also be out of town the day Bernie was murdered. As it turned out, he was transporting prisoners to Menard Prison at the time. Was this also just coincidental . . . or was it convenient, as some people were wondering?

On the day of Bernie's inquest Ashby and Walker decided to tell Sheriff Spainhower all they knew about the Shelton-Gatewood recordings, about Petrakos, Robinson and everything else because they felt it was all connected. They called him out in the hall while the inquest was going on. They thought if they could get Petrakos and the mystery woman to talk, Bernie's murder could be solved.

Spainhower asked to hear the recordings and they met later at the amusement company. After the sheriff heard the recordings, he said maybe they could get more out of Petrakos than he could, but Ashby said they couldn't find him.

The next day the sheriff went on vacation to Canada but apparently failed to tell his chief deputy, Bill Littell. So Ashby also gave Littell the story, who wanted one of his deputies to also hear it and Ashby gave his deputy the highlights.

After that deputy sheriffs Francis and Arends began taking an interest in the case. They told Ashby and Walker that, if they were allowed to make arrests, they could clear up the case in ten hours. They indicated a man had come to them and said he'd give them information regarding the murder. Jack asked them to see if the man was Roy Gatewood and find out if he still had a .351 rifle in his house. He told them Gatewood was an expert rifleman and had a rifle range in his back yard. For some reason, however, they weren't allowed to go out there and question Gatewood. The gang wondered if that was because of Gatewood's friendship with State's Attorney Hull. Ashby claimed the State's Attorney's office made only one investigation into the murder.

Jack couldn't prove it but, after the last recording ended, he said he still had on his headset and heard Gatewood tell Bernie how he was to pay off the $25,000. Hull was to receive the money from Somogyi and Somogyi was to keep some of it to pay off Dr. Rutledge.

Ashby later said Judge Stone called him at the Shelton farm on August 7th. Jack wasn't there, so he called him back at his newspaper office and Stone told him to come right over.

Jack said he told Stone what Petrakos had said about him. Stone responded by saying that, on Wednesday, the day before Bernie's funeral, Pete called him and asked him to come over to his apartment and the Judge's wife dropped him off in her car.

As he entered the apartment he noticed that Pete had a gun lying on the table. Then he told Stone he had something to tell him that wasn't very pleasant. He confessed that he had been a stooge for Clyde Garrison for a number of years and had been telling Clyde everything the Sheltons did and everything that Stone did.

Then he suggested that, now that Bernie was dead, Stone should make up with Garrison and they all could make money in Peoria. Stone said he was so surprised that he left in a hurry.

But before he left Pete told him that, when he left town in July, he was 900 miles from Peoria and only Clyde Garrison knew where he was. He told Stone that he knew when Bernie was killed because Clyde called him and said, "the big boy is gone," and he immediately drove back to Peoria.

Chapter 16

Bernie's Number Came Up Nine Months After Carl's!

An examination of Bernie's body at the hospital showed the bullet struck him near the heart and passed through his body, coming out the right side.

Members of the Shelton family were stunned by the news of Bernie Shelton's death. His 82-year-old mother said, "Who did it, that dirty dog who killed Carl?"

It was reported that Ray Walker, who had been sticking close to Fairfield since the assault in the Parkway, and "Little" Earl Shelton, went to Mt. Vernon and boarded a chartered plane to Peoria. Mrs. Lula Pennington, a sister of the Sheltons, said Bernie's funeral would be held at Fairfield, where Carl had been buried. But Bernie's widow, Genevieve, decided to hold his funeral in Peoria.

Bernie's body was taken to the Boland Mortuary at 300 North Perry, where it was prepared for burial. The next day it was moved to the Shelton farm on Farmington Road where friends and relatives gathered from 3 p.m. to late night, offering their condolences. They were cheered by the news that Bernie's mother, Agnes, would come to Peoria for the funeral.

Many other cars bearing the idly curious turned off Farmington Road into the lane leading to Golden Rule Farm. After reaching the entrance, most of the cars hesitated a few moments, while the people looked at the big white house, then backed out and drove back to the highway.

On the wide screened porch at the rear, women relatives and friends congregated quietly as the men gathered in another room next to the one where Bernie's body lay in the expensive bronze casket, similar to the one in which his brother, Carl, was buried just nine months before. In contrast to the way he lived, Bernie's body now appeared to lay quiet and peaceful, with his hands folded across his lower chest and with his glasses in place. The body rested in an expensive brown pin-striped suit.

Dozens of floral pieces surrounded the casket, some with silk ribbons saying "Our Pal" and "Our Partner."

It was reported that one of Bernie's closest pals denied that Shelton was seeking to "branch out." He said, "His greatest interest was right here on his farm and in his horses."

The rest of the Shelton clan in Fairfield came for the funeral, including his 82-year-old mother. The funeral service was held on Thursday, July 29 at 1:30 p.m. in the chapel at the Boland Mortuary. Shortly before that the $2,500 bronze casket was transferred to the mortuary chapel with only the family members and ranking members of the gang in the small cortege.

An overflow crowd of several hundred persons filled the four reception rooms and halls of the funeral home and the curb outside was lined with curious spectators. A tremendous number of flowers were received shortly before the services and the family asked for them to go directly to hospitals. Even so, it required four trucks to take flowers from the mortuary to the cemetery.

The sermon was given by Reverend E. L. Fernandes of the Arcadia Avenue Presbyterian Church in Peoria and while he spoke, a shorthand reporter in the mezzanine, hired by the Shelton family, made a transcription of the remarks. Then the funeral procession moved to Parkview Cemetery, where Bernie Shelton's body was finally laid to rest.

Ray Walker was reportedly taking over the direction of the Shelton enterprises in Peoria after Bernie's death.

The *St. Louis Post-Dispatch* had previously reported that a $20,000 offer had been made by the Chicago-St. Louis gambling organization for the killing of any leading members of the Shelton gang. The day after Bernie's death, the newspaper said the "reward" was decided on eight weeks before, at the Hyde Park gambling casino in Venice, Illinois, and was now due to be paid.

A few days after Bernie was killed, Jack Ashby and "Big" Earl Shelton had a meeting with Ted Link at the Parkway office. Ray Walker and "Little" Earl were there, too, and they played the Shelton/Gatewood records for Link.

The reporter recognized the one voice on the tape as Roy Gatewood because of his southern accent. He came from Memphis where he was in a carnival with his wife, Dixie.

Link also found that Roy had run away with the daughter of Jake Hammond, a famous murderer down there. But his wife found him and brought him back. Link decided to have a private meeting with State's Attorney Hull. He told Hull he had information given to him by the Sheltons, and asked Hull if he had any evidence left behind by Bernie. Hull said he hadn't.

Hull told him he wasn't supposed to do anything about the recordings and ask him why the *Post-Dispatch* came up here trying to scare him? Link replied he had evidence which involved him and wanted to get at the truth. Hull retaliated by saying the *Post-Dispatch* couldn't intimidate him. With this, Link asked him what he should tell his paper and Hull said he could tell them anything he wanted. Link said that was the last time he saw Hull.

When Link reported the results of his meeting with the State's Attorney, his paper told him to check into the background of Hull's office. Link reported back that the office's handling of the Snooks Gordon murder case of killing a man in a traffic fight, looked a little suspicious and so did an abortion case by a Dr. Rutledge. Link also looked into a case of an influential man who was accused of fooling with little girls, which was never tried. Link also compiled a list of places in Peoria that were operating "wide open."

Later the Shelton group came down to Links hotel room and gave him a copy of the Shelton/Gatewood records to take back to St. Louis. But there was an election going on in St. Louis at the time, and his editors didn't have time to hear them until the following week. After they played them at KSD-Radio there, Link returned to Peoria. Now the Sheltons gave him the original records, thinking they'd be safer in the hands of the *Post-Dispatch*.

Link had been looking for Gatewood, visiting his house six or eight times without success until one morning about 2 a.m. He told Gatewood he wanted to know the truth about him and a "certain official" but Roy told him there was no such connection and said he wouldn't talk to him until later that morning. Link left and returned about 9 a.m. to find that Gatewood was gone again. Link later learned he went to Jack Adams' place in Brainerd, Minnesota.

When Link couldn't find him, he went back to the house to talk to his wife, but she wouldn't come to the door, She yelled out to him that her attorney advised her not to talk or it would get in the paper. Link found out later she never had a lawyer.

Ted Link talked to Claude Stone of the *Peoria Star* right after he talked to Hull and Gatewood, wanting to know what Stone knew about Pete Petrakos. Stone said he thought Pete was a minor racketeer and he was also a Garrison man. He said Pete told him he had been working for Garrison for some time, reporting to him on the movements of the Sheltons. No wonder Pete was so nervous. Stone also said Pete told him he went on vacation before Bernie was killed because he was afraid he'd be found out and hurt by the Shelton gang.

Link went to Pete's apartment at Knoxville and McClure, above the Marine Room. Pete wasn't there but his wife said he was downtown at Boulanger's Chili Parlor. Ted went down and found him there.

Petrakos would only say he had talked to the sheriff. Link called Sheriff Spainhower who said Pete had talked about advance information given by Robinson. Link later went back to Pete's apartment and talked to him for two hours but Pete wasn't talking logically and was obviously very nervous.

At this point Link got an idea. If he could get Pete with his former "friends," Ashby, "Big" Earl and Walker, maybe he'd tell them something.

Many of the local gamblers were conspicuous in their absence at Bernie's funeral, and another "friend" who never attended was Johnny Robinson. So, on the night of July 30th, the Friday after Bernie was killed, Link, Ashby, "Big" Earl and Walker met Robinson about

9 p.m. at Duffy's Tavern in Bartonville. They told him they had to know the name of the mystery girl he used to go with because Bernie was now dead. Johnny told them her name was Mary Davis from Little Rock, Arkansas but they'd never find her.

After they left Robinson, they drove out to Petrakos' apartment but they didn't go in. They decided that Ashby should go to a pay phone and call Petrakos, suggesting that he meet him downtown to discuss the *St. Louis Post-Dispatch* matter. Pete said he didn't have a car but Ashby said it was important that he talk to him, and to call a taxi.

Then the four drove back downtown and parked in front of the Pere Marquette hotel. The other three waited in the car for Pete to show up while Link went on up to his room.

Ashby and Walker got out of the car as they spotted Pete across the street. Earl stayed in the car. When Pete came across to the hotel Ashby and Walker walked up behind him, while Earl got out and joined them. With Ashby on one side and Walker on the other, (Pete claimed Walker put something hard in his side) they walked him into the hotel and went up to Links room.

Link said he asked Pete if he minded going over the thing again and said Pete gave him names of people and places where he had been. He also asked him about a girl he dated but Pete claimed he didn't have a girl and he was happily married. Link indicated Pete was very nervous when Ashby asked him some questions and Pete jumped up on the bed and chain-smoked cigarettes but didn't answer.

Pete said they pushed him around and roughed him up but the others denied it. Ashby accused him of telling the girl about the meeting he had set up at Ashby's house to play the recordings to Judge Stone that was later cancelled. This was where she said the first attempt to kill Bernie was to occur. If it failed, the plan was to get him on his trip to Iowa.

Ashby told Pete it had to be him because there were only three people who knew about Bernie's trip, Bernie, Pete and himself. But Pete denied it by saying a fourth party knew . . . Judge Stone!

Since they were getting nowhere, Link said the conversation became more friendly and they had some drinks. They remained in Link's room until 3 a.m. Both Ashby and Walker offered to drive Pete home, but he refused and hurriedly left.

Later Link talked to Sheriff Spainhower, asking if he had made any progress in finding Bernie's killer. The sheriff said he'd just gotten back from vacation and wasn't as yet familiar with the case as he should be.

Jack Ashby told Link that Charles Somogyi, chief investigator of the State's Attorney office; Peoria County liquor commissioner, Roscoe Zerwekh; and Illinois state commissioner, Fisher were getting a payoff and George Chiames, a Shelton "bag man" was also getting something. Chiames supposedly also had contacts in Chicago with state officers.

Harry Tyrell was paying out all the pay-off money. Link thought Harry was a smart operator but his only fault was keeping a record book of the money for years. Link indicated there was also an anonymous letter sent to Mrs. Agnes Shelton, the mother of the Shelton boys, postmarked July 27, 1948, the day after Bernie was killed. It said, "Mrs. Shelton: Positively Clyde Garrison and Snooks Gordon know who killed Bernie. Destroy this letter and spare my life." It was signed: "From one who knows." and sent to Fairfield, Illinois.

At Fairfield, "Big" Earl Shelton blamed Bernie's murder on the failure of law enforcement officers to find the killers of their brother, Carl. He said, "The law could have prevented Bernie's murder if they had solved Carl's killing. I'm through talking. I talked my head off after Carl was killed but what's the use? We get no protection from the law, so we are trying to watch out for ourselves."

Earl told a newspaper reporter that he was busy managing his large farm and had "no time for anything else." He said he recently heard that Charley Harris, who was suspected by the Sheltons to be the fingerman in Carl Shelton's murder, was "laying" for him. Earl stated, "He has been seen near my place in the last three weeks, one time dressed in women's clothing."

After Bernie's assassination, it was reported that the next victims on the gangsters' hit list were "Big" Earl Shelton and Ray Walker.

Shortly after Bernie's murder, the *Post-Dispatch* reported it had been learned that the St. Louis-Chicago syndicate had called on leaders of the Shelton gang in Peoria two months before, in an effort to settle differences over the control of gambling. The paper said the representatives of the syndicate brought word from the group, headed by Frank "Buster" Wortman of East St. Louis, that they were willing to make peace if the Sheltons forgot about reprisals for the murder of Carl Shelton. But now, with Bernie's death it was obvious that someone out there still wasn't in a peace-making mood.

One man who was obviously pleased to have both Sheltons out of the way was Clyde Garrison. Clyde was unhappy from the start of the Shelton's Peoria reign. Now he would be free to become more active in the gambling picture in Illinois, and it didn't take him long to make a move.

On August 14, 1948, less than a month after Bernie Shelton was killed, Ted Link reported that Garrison was now representing the Chicago Capone syndicate's gambling wire service in four Illinois counties.

Link said he is the man in charge of placing the new "baseball" tickers in hideaway gambling establishments in recent weeks. He also stated that Garrison is a frequent passenger in the Illinois State patrol car of Captain Thomas E. Murphy.

Appearance of the tickers, which carry the results of major league baseball games, horse races and other sports events on which there is betting, came into the Peoria area about the time Bernie was killed.

Shelton followers who saw some significance in the coincidence in view of the fact that the Shelton and Garrison groups had been rivals for years, say they had heard nothing about the tickers until after Bernie's death.

The appearance of the baseball tickers, with Garrison in charge in Peoria, Tazewell, Mason and Fulton counties indicates the Capone interests, which the Sheltons resisted bitterly in Central and Southern Illinois, had taken over organized wire service into Peoria.

The wire service for the new tickers was from Chicago direct. A gambling house in Orchard mines with one of the new tickers was raided the afternoon of August 12 by sheriff's deputies and they found 30 customers in the place and retrieved evidence of them betting on a horse race. The proprietor was placed under a $1,500 bond pending a hearing on the charge.

Ted Link's article also stated that George Chiames had been known for years to the Peoria area as "the man from the state" to distinguish him from the other graft collectors for the county and municipal officials. When a slot machine man asked Chiames where the money he collected went, George answered "to Chicago."

It was claimed George Chiames had been a collector of graft "for the state" since 1941 or 1942. That would coincide with the time Carl Shelton was invited into Peoria to become the new "kingpin" of gambling to replace Garrison and, within the past years he and Bernie Shelton, with others, had flooded the surrounding area with punchboards.

This didn't prove very profitable, however, due partly to monthly payoffs to two county officials and $1.00 a month to Chiames "for the state" on each board. Also, the county officials each received $2.00 a month for every board in operation. Chiames told Link he also had "a federal connection in Washington D.C." and also denied knowing anything about slot machine payoffs. He claimed his other business, besides running a pool hall, was "handling investments." This article also stated that an East St. Louis gambler said he also traced his payoffs to Chicago.

Another *Post-Dispatch* story claimed that Chiames was on the payroll of the Illinois Attorney General's office in Chicago at about $400 a month. A first assistant to Attorney General George F. Barrett said that he had hired Chiames on his own without knowing anything about him. He claimed he hired him as a sales tax investigator. Link said Chiames was carried on the state payroll until August 15, 1948. He said Shelton associates told him that Chiames had collected $200 in monthly graft from the Pair-a-Dice Club alone, of which the Sheltons owned a 30 percent share.

But by mid-August 1948, it was reported that George Chiames had been missing from Peoria for about a month.

In those dangerous days it was sometimes healthy to be missing from Peoria!

But whatever the future would be for Clyde Garrison continuing in the rackets, it probably didn't last long. He retired not many years later and was in failing health for many of those years and spent much time in sanitariums before entering Methodist Hospital in Peoria, where he died quietly in bed on June 12, 1959.

Chapter 17

Is "Big" Earl Next?

In the later 1940's, Peoria had a weekly newspaper that wanted to compete with the two daily papers, the *Peoria Journal-Transcript* and the *Peoria Star*. It started out as a weekly shopping guide under the name of the *Peoria Shopping News,* but it had since changed its name by dropping the word "shopping" from its title to, simply, *Peoria News.* It was started by Bill Oakley, a former editor of the *Peoria Star* and Jim Coogan, a former advertising salesman for that paper. The name change was an effort to sound more competitive.

In its issue of September 30, 1948, it had found another way to compete with the daily papers. That day its headlines screamed, "Publisher Accused!" and "Claude U. Stone Editor and Publisher of Peoria Star, Named by Petrakos as 'Mystery Man' Who Received $600 Monthly Payoffs from Shelton Gang."

Its lead story continued with Peter J. Petrakos' statement to the grand jury, in which he linked Stone with both Carl and Bernie Shelton, and that he, Stone, had been receiving payoffs from the gang.

Petrakos stated he had been friendly with Carl Shelton and had sold punch boards for him. He said he had met Carl in Bill DeGaris' tavern before he was drafted into the Army in 1943. After Carl was killed, he was contacted by Bernie Shelton and he introduced Claude Stone to Bernie. He stated he had witnessed one payoff and saw twelve $50 bills in another envelope he delivered from Bernie to Stone.

As late as September 29, 1949, the *Peoria News* was still screaming about the fact that Bernie Shelton's murder had never been solved, with headlines such as, "Shelton Case Called A 'Family Affair' By Some," "Shelton Case Becoming Triangle," "SHELTON KILLING LAID TO 'RELATIVE,'" "Hopes For Gamblers 'Blasted' By Courts," and as late as March 1950 the weekly paper was still shouting "WHO KILLED BERNIE SHELTON?" Maybe it helped to sell papers, but it's highest hopes of solving the case never materialized.

After Bernie's killing, it was generally reported that "Big" Earl Shelton and Ray Walker would be next on the death list if the Shelton's tried to hold its territory against the Chicago-St. Louis gambling syndicate.

The Capone gang of Chicago and the Egan gang of St. Louis had merged before the two Shelton brothers had been killed. It was obvious they wanted the downstate Illinois territory and would eliminate the Sheltons if they had to. They had reportedly offered $20,000 for Bernie's removal after Carl had been taken out.

Earl Shelton had left Peoria and gone back to live on his farm near Fairfield. On May 24, 1949, the year after Bernie was killed, "Big" Earl took a bullet near the heart from a shot fired through a window in his gambling den, The Farmer's Club, on the east side of the square, across from the Wayne County Courthouse in Fairfield. The club occupied the second floor of the building, above a restaurant on the square.

It was about 10:20 p.m., when three shots were fired through a second-story window in the rear of the club.

It was estimated later that the shots were fired from about 60 feet at an angle through the window near which Shelton was sitting. Someone had climbed to the roof of a one-story building that housed the Hoffee Motor Company, next to the club. The window was the only one that was not blacked out in Earl's semi-private club. The rear of the "Hoffee" building extended beyond the rear of the Shelton building and the gunman was obviously familiar with this fact.

"Big" Earl's brother, Dalta, and his two sons, "Little" Earl and "Little" Carl, were also in town and both boys were in the club at the time of the shooting. "Little" Carl said, "Uncle Earl was sitting there, just talking, when he got shot. He'd been playing poker but had laid down his hand and gone to the serving counter."

"Little" Earl said he was alone in the front room of the social club when he heard the shots. He said there was only a handful of people there and, "If they'd waited three more minutes we'd been gone."

He said "Big" Earl was sitting on a stool at the counter with his back to the window. "I looked in the other room when I heard the shots and everybody was on the floor, crawling toward the front room. I didn't know anyone had been shot until Uncle Earl walked into the room—he was the only one standing up."

A ladder was later found lying against the back of the garage, and was examined for fingerprints. Sheriff Harlan said that Shelton was hit by one bullet from a glancing blow. It had struck a molding on the edge of the counter and entered Earl's back. Other bullets found at the scene indicated that they came from a .43-caliber pistol, probably of Spanish make.

The ambulance dashed Shelton to the home of Dr. Frankel in Fairfield, who directed them to his office. He administered emergency treatment and the ambulance then took Earl to Deaconess Hospital in Evansville,

Indiana, about 70 miles away. There, a Dr. Visher worked on Shelton from about 1:00 a.m. until nearly dawn. He said the bullet entered the body near the center of the back and passed through, breaking a front left rib, which caused it to glance upward, lodging under the shoulder. Because the bullet was located so near to the heart, the doctor decided to leave it in him, unless it caused trouble later.

After the surgery, Earl's wife, Earline, stayed with him in his room while his nephew, "Little" Earl, patrolled the hall outside his door.

At the time of the shooting, Earl was involved in a local political argument over whether Wayne County should remain "dry" or be voted "wet," with regard to selling liquor. Although "Big" Earl had been a bootlegger in the old days of Prohibition, he was now in favor of a "wet" county because liquor was now legal in "wet" counties and he had plans to open a saloon on the ground floor of his building. He also had obtained options on several other likely tavern sites.

Two weeks before this latest shooting, a mass meeting was held in Fairfield's Christian Church and they formed a Fairfield Civic League to fight to keep the town dry.

The "drys" won the town election after pamphlets denouncing the Sheltons and the Penningtons, who were Earl's sister Lula's in-laws. The pamphlets were dropped by plane over Wayne County.

The pamphlet read:

"One: The Shelton-Pennington gang and other ex-convicts are managing the WET campaign and distributing the distiller's and brewer's money to vote saloons 'in' in Fairfield.

"Two: The Shelton-Pennington gang have already rented and taken options on buildings in the city in which to run saloons if the city votes wet.

"Three: Saloons operated by gangs and gangsters

attract other gangs and gangsters from everywhere. They become the centers of gang warfare and murders. They are the laboratories of murders, robberies, sex crimes and every other criminal activity.

"Four: Vote DRY and protect Wayne county and Fairfield from a Williamson county and Herrin recollection and protect our women and children from sex attacks.

"Facts the voters of Fairfield should not forget in voting on the wet and dry issue."

(Signed) "DRY COMMITTEE."

Despite the linking of the Sheltons and Penningtons in the pamphlet, it had recently been reported that "Big" Earl had already had a falling out with his sister Lula and her husband, Guy Pennington. He suspected they were working with the "drys" because of Guy's known bootlegging interests, which would be seriously affected by a return of legal liquor.

On May 14, 1949, ten days before the shooting of "Big" Earl, the front windows of the Pennington's Fairfield home were shot out by gunmen in a passing automobile. Guy Pennington's uncle, Taylor Pennington, was also recently assaulted and severely beaten. Shots were also fired into a parked car and into a county cafe as the violence mounted to open warfare.

It was also thought that "Big" Earl had quarreled with other relatives over property that had been left by Carl and Bernie. He argued with Bernie's widow, Genevieve Shelton, over property in Peoria and Florida and he was said to have had a dispute with Ray Walker who succeeded Bernie as the boss of the Shelton gang.

"Big" Earl Shelton lived through his near fatal shooting, but the bullet was never removed. Less than four months after "Big" Earl's brush with death, "Little" Earl became the target on September 9, 1949. He was ambushed as he parked his car in front of his five-room frame house at 112 W. Elm Street in Fairfield. He was shot eight times as he sat in his Buick. "Little" Earl threw himself on the floor of the car as 21 bullets riddled the front door on the driver's side and this action probably saved his life. Two bullet holes were made from the inside of the car, indicating that Earl had fired back.

Aided by his wife, Eleanor, he crawled into his house, leaving a trail of blood behind him. A Fairfield city policeman, Elmo Musgrave, found him there a few minutes later. He was taken to Deaconess Hospital in Evansville, Indiana, in the same Dixon and Crippen ambulance that took his uncle, "Big" Earl to this same hospital the previous May.

He was immediately taken to surgery and the doctor was still working on him when his uncle and namesake, and his brother, "Little" Carl, got to the hospital. There were ten places where bullets had gone into, or out of, his body. Two bullets were left in him; one in the left thigh and one in the left hip. Later, "Big" Earl stayed just outside the door of his room, the same as "Little" Earl had done for him the previous May.

This Earl also ultimately recovered from his wounds. He and his wife had two daughters at the time of the ambush.

While his father, Dalta, had never been identified with the Shelton gang, the son had been named in connection with Shelton gambling enterprises in Illinois.

"Little" Earl admitted he fired back at the car that had attacked him and gave authorities the license number and a description of it. His identification of the car checked out to be a red Pontiac convertible owned by Charley Harris, the same man the Sheltons previously believed had fingered his Uncle Carl. Fairfield police were reluctant to act, however. They doubted that Shelton could see the license plate on the car at night.

When they subsequently took Harris into custody he showed them his car, which had been disabled, and it showed no bullet marks on it.

But Harris was charged with "assault to commit murder" anyway. He made his $5,000 bond and returned to his farm.

On October 20, he was released in the shooting of "Little" Earl, when the Sheltons failed to appear in court. The nephew had apparently decided not to press charges because he felt that the only testimony would be his own and he didn't believe that would be enough to convict Harris.

On May 22, 1950, a little over eight months after "Little" Earl's narrow escape from ambush, both Earls were riding to a Shelton oil well when they were, again, shot at.

Machinegun, shotgun and rifle slugs were sprayed into their car but, miraculously, "Big" Earl was just nicked in the arm, while his nephew escaped uninjured this time.

After this second attempt on "Big" Earl's life within the past year, he vowed to "die with my boots on and take some enemies with me when I go."

When Hal Bradshaw, the Wayne County Sheriff, asked him why he didn't clear out of the Fairfield area, Earl retorted, "Why should I? They'll follow us. We'll make our last stand right here where I belong—right on my own property."

"Little" Earl, who had survived 10 bullet wounds previously, was also incensed. He shouted, "Call in the FBI. Get the state troopers. We'll fix those guys. We know who they are." But when the sheriff asked for names, he refused to answer.

The slug that hit "Big" Earl in the right arm had

whizzed past his nephew who was driving. He said the gunfire kept up as he pushed the accelerator to the floor and roared away from the scene. His uncle was treated at the Frankel-Marx Clinic in Fairfield and released.

This attempt occurred near the Pond Creek farm where Carl was gunned down in October 1947.

Then fourteen days later, on June 5, 1950, "Little" Earl Shelton, was involved in yet another ambush. This time he was with Deloss Wylie.

This was the fourth attempt to kill "Little" Earl, who was not hurt but Wylie was seriously wounded. This was also the latest of six shootings in three years involving the Shelton clan.

The attackers had apparently waited in a patch of undergrowth near a garage Shelton and Wylie had recently purchased, four miles west of Fairfield. Deputy Elmer Brown said the weeds were neatly cut on the spot carefully camouflaged from the highway. Shells from hard-boiled eggs were on the ground, which indicated someone waited for them to show up.

The gunmen apparently used a shotgun loaded with deer slugs, and shells from a .30 caliber rifle were also found at the scene. Brown added that a machinegun had also been used.

Shelton was unscathed and his quick action probably saved his life. He ducked behind the doors of his Buick sedan, the same car he was in when he was shot in front of his house the year before.

As he ducked, he shoved Wylie out of the car and the two ran to the garage, using the car as a shield. The gunmen sent a second fusillade into the garage and Wylie was cut down as he attempted to get out the back way. He was shot four times; three times in the chest and once in the elbow. He was taken to the Clay County hospital at Flora, Illinois, where doctors gave him an even chance to survive.

Wylie, 35, was the father of five children and had been associated with the Shelton family for many years. He had been operating a filling station on Highway 45 near Fairfield until he and Earl decided to go into the garage business. Wylie eventually recovered from his wounds.

Chapter 18

Brother Roy's Number Comes Up

On June 7, 1950, just two days after "Little" Earl and Deloss Wylie were ambushed, Carl and Bernie Shelton's older brother, Roy, was assassinated.

At about 6:40 a.m. Roy, 65, the oldest of the five Shelton brothers, was killed by a high-powered rifle shot, while riding a tractor on his farm. The spot was about 200 yards from where his brother, "Big" Earl, and his nephew, "Little" Earl, had escaped an attack two weeks before.

Roy was hit twice; once in the middle of the back and again in the groin. He then fell from the tractor and was run over by the harrow and disc rig he was pulling to cultivate his Pond Creek bottoms farm, 12 miles southeast of Fairfield.

A farm hand, Frank "Whiz" McKibben, about 49, was driving a second tractor about 100 feet away, and was shot at twice when he went to Shelton's aid, but wasn't hit. He said he jumped off his tractor and ran to Roy's rig, shutting off the power. He then took shelter behind a wheel of the tractor and remained there until he thought the assassin had left. He said he saw no one but he then searched the underbrush at the north end of the field, where the gunman had hidden. The tracks indicated that one man had done the shooting.

"Shoddy" Hutchcraft, who worked on Roy's farm, was in a nearby field when he heard the shots. He galloped up on horseback to see what happened, and than rode to notify the family.

Roy was working on the land that had formerly belonged to Carl. The scene was also only about 500 yards north of a Shelton oil well but the oil workers had not yet reported to work that morning. Roy and his wife, Blanche, now lived on the farm. They had no children.

Roy Shelton had no recent record of trouble, although he had served prison time earlier.

After Roy's death, authorities said one discharged shell was found at the scene. It was a Winchester rifle shell made in St. Louis . . . and was reported to be the same type used to kill Bernie Shelton in Peoria, two years earlier.

Roy Shelton was now the third of five Shelton brothers to be slain in less than three years, but his slaying was a surprise to Fairfield residents who said that Roy and Dalta, 50, of Cisne, 14 miles northwest of Fairfield, had not been active in the Shelton gang. Both men had stuck close to their farming.

At the next day's inquest, "Big" Earl was put under the guard of four Illinois State Highway patrolmen. After all, he had already escaped two attacks on his life in just the past year.

The coroner's jury returned what had become a very familiar verdict in Wayne County; "death by gunshot, by person or persons unknown." This would mark the sixth time that Wayne County authorities had failed to develop any leads in six shootings since Carl Shelton's murder in 1947.

The only other living brother, Dalta, remained close to his farm home at Cisne, Illinois, where he had moved to get away from the Pond Creek bottoms, following Carl's assassination.

Roy Shelton's death begged an answer to the obvious question: Where was "Black" Charley Harris?

Harris had reportedly been wintering in Phoenix, Arizona and Wayne County State's Attorney Mayberry wired authorities there. They said he had left there two weeks ago, heading home to Fairfield via Oregon. With this information Mayberry said, "As far as I know, Harris isn't in town. If he was here, I wouldn't hold him. There's nothing in the evidence that indicates he was connected with Roy's shooting."

Roy's funeral was held at 2 p.m. on June 10 at the Dixon-Crippen funeral home where, hours before, friends and curious strangers gathered and milled in and out.

The Reverend Kent M. Dale presided over the services and had an interesting comment in his sermon. He said, "Tragedy again has stalked across our smiling fields . . . I do not intend to be a master of ceremonies at a show, but a minister of Jesus."

After the service, as about three hundred people looked on, Roy's widow, Blanche, was embracing another woman as she left and Roy's mother was sobbing hysterically.

Roy was buried at Maple Hill Cemetery, where his father, Benjamin, and brother, Carl, were buried.

But this day was not over . . .

Roy Shelton was buried on June 10, 1950, and ***on that same night,*** the violence against the Sheltons continued. Someone tried to burn down the gas station where "Little" Earl and Deloss Wylie narrowly escaped death the week before. The man who sold the garage to them discovered the blaze as he returned to pick up some furniture.

State Police Sgt. Charles Rudesill, one of the three officers who answered the call, said he smelled gasoline on the walls of the building. They put out the fire with water from a nearby well before it did any serious damage.

But strange things were also happened to Carl's widow, Pearl Vaughan Shelton, who was still living in Peoria.

Carl had been killed in October 1947 and Bernie was killed the following year, in July 1948. But in the summers of 1949 and 1950, she was still receiving weird telegrams from both of them, *even though they were dead!* The telegrams were sent to her address at 1308 Knoxville.

The first one was dated May 22, 1949 and said, "WE WILL BE SEEING YOU AND AL SOON. IT CAN'T BE LONG NOW. (signed) BERNIE AND CARL." The second one was dated the following year, July 12, 1950, and said, "SORRY YOU AND AL WERE OUT FRIDAY SATURDAY AND TODAY. WILL CALL WHEN WE GET BACK. (signed) CARL AND BERNIE."

All of this had Pearl nearly out of her mind with fright. She was so scared she couldn't sleep at night and could hardly keep food on her stomach. At this point Pearl's attorney gave her some personal advice that probably saved her life. With all the underlying things that were going on and, not knowing who was behind it, he told her to get out of town before someone decided that the next Shelton to die should be her.

So, on August 15, 1951, Pearl gave him her "power of attorney," packed her bags and headed for Oakland, California to live with an aunt.

Much speculation was going on regarding the shooting of the Sheltons and many theories were forwarded. Everything from: old enemies from the East St. Louis bootlegging days, to the Williamson County war days, to the Peoria gambling days. One of the more prominent theories, as mentioned before, was that the

Chicago-St. Louis syndicate was unhappy with them and wanted their gambling territory.

But a new theory was raised in June 1950 by the *Chicago Herald-American* newspaper. Their theory was that oil had been recently discovered in the Pond Creek bottoms and their enemies were determined that the Shelton clan would not enjoy their good fortune.

The first well was brought in in 1947. The fourth well in the area was brought in just before Roy Shelton's death in 1950. It was named the "Earl Shelton No. 1," and was producing 300 barrels of oil a day.

But why didn't the Shelton's fight back, the Chicago paper asked? The *Herald-American* theorized that it was because they were powerless. They could fight an underworld gang, but they couldn't wage war against an aroused army of citizens who were fed up with lawlessness. But this was not to be the end of the Shelton family's problems.

In November 1950, "Big" Earl's home was destroyed by a tin-can bomb and, in June 1951, an ambusher wounded E. H. O. Daniels, Jr., 28, as he was farming "Big" Earl's land on a lease basis, and two days later, Earl's barn was burned to the ground.

The Pennington's; the Shelton boys sister, Lula, and her husband, Guy, also had their share of fire and bombs. In 1950, bombs wrecked their new $10,000 roadhouse and their nearby restaurant. The next night a fire, which had apparently been deliberately set, burned the damaged roadhouse to the ground.

It became even more obvious. Someone still wanted the Shelton family out of the way . . . ***real bad!***

Chapter 19

Somebody Wanted More Than Just

The Shelton "Brothers"

By January 1951, "Big" and "Little" Earl had apparently had enough. They quietly packed up their families and left Wayne County without telling anyone where they were going. The fifth brother, Dalta, had already left in the summer of 1950.

Now, only the Shelton's mother, Mrs. Agnes Shelton, matriarch of the clan, along with her daughter, Lula, 42, and Lula's husband, Guy Pennington, 37, continued to live in Fairfield.

The next action against the Shelton family occurred on June 28, 1951, when the Penningtons were wounded by a lone gunman on a Fairfield city street. They described their attacker as a wildly laughing man yielding a machine-gun.

Lula was the last Shelton sibling still defying what had become a local vendetta, intended to exterminate the entire family. All the other Shelton brothers and sisters were either dead or had been put to flight.

Three hours after the Penningtons were shot, Louis Sons, 56, a laborer, was found dead with two bullet wounds in his body at a resort owned by Guy

Pennington's brother, Ogie. Bootleg liquor was reportedly sold there, three miles south of Fairfield in the dry county. Later, Ogie Pennington was accused of the murder of Sons.

The Penningtons named their assailant as "Black" Charley Harris, 55, the ex-convict and former Shelton gangster. Magistrate W. A. Hill sent a deputy to Guy's hospital bed where he signed a complaint against Harris and authorities issued a warrant charging Harris with assault with intent to commit murder.

There was a sharp disagreement between witnesses to the shooting as to whether or not the gunman was Harris, but Assistant State's Attorney William Pierce said he had four witnesses who said it was.

But State's Attorney Gerald Mayberry said that Sam Mercer, a resident at the scene, saw the shooting from his yard and reported that the gunman was a large, bushy-haired man who used two pistols. Harris was small and slick-haired and the Penningtons said he used a drum-type machinegun.

In their account of the shooting, the Penningtons said they were driving home from a grocery store about 11 a.m., when a car approached from the opposite direction and blocked their passage at an intersection on the west side of town.

They said it was Harris and his niece, Beatrice (Jakie) Bell Suddarth, in the car. These two were also previously reported to be together near the scene of the killing of Carl Shelton in 1947.

The Penningtons said Harris took a machinegun from his car and wounded them both with a burst of bullets. When Lula staggered from the car and stumbled to a nearby patch of weeds, she said Harris followed her but his gun jammed. As he slapped the gun to get it to resume firing, Lula said he ignored her pleas not to shoot and told her, "I'm going to kill all the Sheltons, just like I did your brothers. And I'm going to cut your mother up in little pieces and throw her around the county." Lula said, when he got the gun operating again, he fired more shots at her on the ground, inflicting additional wounds, a total of six in all.

In the meantime Guy leaped from the car and started running, according to their account. He said Harris turned the gun on him but it jammed again and, before he could jar it loose, his brother, Ogie, drove up, which prompted Harris to leap into his own car and flee.

The wounded couple was taken to the County Memorial Hospital, three blocks from the scene. They were reported in serious condition but were expected to live. Guy had received four bullet wounds himself.

In contradiction to the Pennington's "positive identification," Assistant State's Attorney Pierce said that a service station attendant on Illinois Route 15, six miles from Fairfield, stated that Harris and Jakie drove their black Mercury sedan into his station to buy gasoline ten minutes before the time the Penningtons were taken to the hospital.

Pierce said, "We're considering this as an alibi which must be proved. But we're still charging Harris with the assault."

Harris surrendered the following day on a charge of attempting to kill the Penningtons but he was freed on $10,000 bond.

Observers noted the similarity between the accusations made against Harris in this shooting and the slaying of Carl Shelton. In both cases he admittedly was at the scene, or within a few miles of it, and was accompanied by his niece. In both cases, Shelton witnesses quoted conversations with him at the scene, indicating positive identification but there was no other proof.

So now, with all of the other Sheltons either dead or

gone to quieter places, only the mother remained unscathed by the scourge believed aimed at annihilating the entire family.

On June 30, two days after the fatal shooting of Louis Sons, Guy Pennington's roadhouse was set afire and burned to the ground. The tavern had been closed since the shooting.

Then, on July 6, 1951, "Big" Earl's tenant, Hillardy O'Daniel, Jr., was wounded by a hidden gunman. He was hit in the arm by one of three slugs fired from ambush while he stood talking to two farmhands. The gunman escaped but the wound was not considered serious. The vendetta against the Sheltons had apparently become so violent that it wasn't even safe to work for one of them.

The handwriting must have been on the wall as far as the rest of the Shelton family was concerned, too. Twelve days later the *St. Louis Post-Dispatch* reported that the day before, Lula Shelton Pennington and her husband had slipped away from the Fairfield Memorial Hospital, where they were recovering from gunshot wounds. They had also apparently taken Lula's 85-year-old mother with them.

It was stated that the Penningtons paid their hospital bill in full, and left at dawn of July 17, in a taxicab summoned from Princeton, Indiana, just across the state line.

The Penningtons had already put their home up for "immediate sale," which ended the Shelton family's 60-year reign in Wayne County.

"Big" Earl and his wife, Earline, along with "Little" Earl and his family, had left earlier and were also said to be living in Indiana. It was thought that Dalta and his family, who had left his farm at Cisne, Illinois in 1950, were also located there.

On July 27, it was reported that the charges against

Charles "Black Charley" Harris for gunning down Lula and Guy Pennington, were dismissed. Harris' attorney, Kelley Loy, had demanded a dismissal of the charges for lack of prosecution. State's Attorney Gerald Mayberry apparently had no choice but to drop them because he said he had no word from the Penningtons since they quietly left the hospital. It was not known where they were but Mother Shelton had also disappeared, and it would seem that all three had decided to join the rest of the surviving Shelton family elsewhere.

But the vengeance against the family didn't stop here. There had been a report that "Big" Earl would return under state protection but the following year, on March 29, 1952, a tenant's house on Earl's 900-acre Hilltop Farm was burned to the ground by arsonists, along with the vacated home of Ray Walker, the Shelton's friend and former gang member.

These fires completed the job of wiping out all the buildings on "Big" Earl's farm; his home, and two barns having been destroyed earlier. Also, three months before this latest torching, flames had also destroyed the Shelton's mother's home. Sheriff Elmer Brown stated the obvious, "This is just proof that they are not going to let "Big" Earl come back and operate the farm." Brown said he didn't know who "they" were but he "wouldn't want to farm it as long as the Sheltons own it."

The farm hadn't been worked since its last tenant, Hillardy O'Daniel, Jr. was wounded by a hidden gunman the previous July, and no attempt had been made to harvest the past year's crop.

It appeared that both of these fires had been set at about the same time. Neighbors near the farm found the tenant home fire and reported it. They gathered to watch it burn but made no attempt to put it out. Sheriff Brown and a newspaper reporter discovered the Walker home fire while on the way to the other one. Walker's place was completely furnished and had been quickly abandoned by him about a year-and-a-half before, after Roy Shelton was killed. The local people who watched it slowly burn also lacked a desire to help put it out. Comments were made that the rural area had no water lines, so they were helpless to do anything.

Walker's home sat on a three-acre tract of land cut out of "Big" Earl's farm. Ray had repeatedly tried to sell it but he had no offers, nor was he able to stir any interest through an ad he ran in the local newspaper.

"Big" Earl had allegedly attempted to obtain protection from state authorities through a St. Louis newspaper reporter who said he had received a telephone call from Earl in a nearby state. He and "Little" Earl had been reported living in trailers in Kentucky and Indiana.

The reporter said Earl asked him to appeal to Governor Adlai Stevenson for help, so that he could come back and farm his land. The governor's office, however, said it had received no such request.

Earl insisted that his nemesis, "Black Charley" Harris, had been patrolling his farm on horseback, armed with a shotgun, and also covering nearby roads by car with a machinegun. Sheriff Brown scoffed at these statements, however. He said that, for several weeks, Harris had been on a trip to southern states. Others were wondering if Harris had been hunting down the fleeing Shelton family.

So, was this finally the end of the vendetta against the Sheltons?

Not Quite! Because the Sheltons still owned one more piece of property in town ***that hadn't, as yet, been destroyed!***

Chapter 20

Charley Is Still Up To His "Black" Deeds

In the early morning hours of Tuesday, July 15, 1952, the now sleepy town of Fairfield was rocked by the explosion of a bomb blast at the two-story brick building owned by "Big" Earl Shelton on the town's public square. The building had formerly housed The Farmer's Club, the gambling den of the Sheltons and the place where "Big" Earl was shot and nearly killed in May 1949.

Most of Fairfield's 6,000 residents were rudely awakened by the blast and hundreds hastened to the scene. Sheriff Elmer Brown said an explosive had apparently been placed at the front door of a restaurant that had just opened the day before. Two adjoining garages were damaged and windows were shattered in buildings two blocks away.

The blast wrecked the interior of the restaurant and knocked out plaster on the second floor. Brown estimated the damage to the building at $10,000.

The sheriff said he had run barefoot to the public square, thinking the Fairfield National Bank had been blown up. A local attorney, Randall Quindry, had recently contracted to buy the building from Earl Shelton through an out-of-town agent but the sale had not been completed. The next episode in the Shelton drama occurred a couple months later, on September 10, 1952, when Ogie Pennington, Guy Pennington's brother, was freed of the murder charge in the killing of Louis Sons, a laborer, in Ogie's saloon, as mentioned earlier. The murder had occurred the same day that Guy and Lula Pennington had been gunned down in June 1951.

Three prosecution witnesses had testified that they saw Ogie Pennington and Louis Sons together at Ogie's resort when they went there to buy whisky shortly before the killing.

Even as late as 1952, it seemed dangerous for anyone who had even bought Shelton family property. Carl Shelton's widow, Pearl Vaughan Shelton, had sold Carl's 1,000-acre farm, and on September 17, 1952, Don "Bud" Newman, 21, a farmhand and brother of Ralph Newman, a half owner of the farm, was wounded in the left arm as he rode a bulldozer while clearing trees.

After Newman was taken to the Fairfield hospital and released, he reportedly left town after telling Sheriff Brown that he had been fired on five times from ambush.

By the early 1950's, the Sheltons were all either killed off or scared off, but their old nemesis, Charley Harris, certainly wasn't. He was still acting like the "Black Charley" of old, well into the next decade.

In 1960, Harris had a run-in with oil operators. He said they were spoiling his soybean farming with digging operations on farmland he owned, which once was the property of "Big" Earl Shelton.

Harris had posted the property with "no trespassing" signs and he had talked of enforcing them with a gun, if necessary. Charley said he had bought the land from a man who purchased it from Earl Shelton, but the oil rights to the land were believed to be still held by Earl.

Then on January 5, 1963, Charley Harris was wounded in the forearm by a 22-caliber pistol shot.

Shortly before noon he drove himself to the office of Dr. David Gershenson and said he was shot by an unknown man. But his neighbor and former friend, Howard S. Taylor, 74, was found dead in his car three-quarters of a mile south of Harris' farm home. The two men had been friends for many years until three years before, when they started having trouble. And about a month before this latest shooting, Taylor won a $1,000 judgment in Wayne County Circuit Court after charging that Harris' hogs had damaged his corn.

Mrs. Taylor told a newsman her husband had left home about 11 a.m. to go to Fairfield. She then heard shots and, a short time later, Taylor's body was found slumped over the steering wheel of his car. The windshield wipers were still running.

Sheriff Leathers found a 22-caliber pistol under Taylor with five shots fired from the weapon. Thirteen bullet holes were in his car. The sheriff also said he found some big-game rifle slugs, 45-caliber shells and shotgun wadding. The shooting took place on a gravel road, four miles east of Fairfield.

Indictments were returned on the night of January 18 against Harris and Willie Hutchcraft, 40, by a Wayne County grand jury probing the death of Taylor. Hutchcraft, who had a record of misdemeanor arrests, lived with his mother at Golden Gate, a community about 15 miles from Fairfield. Both men were jailed pending setting of bonds. The press was not allowed to read the indictments and its exact wording was not known.

At his trial for the murder of Howard Taylor, Harris testified that Taylor had fired the first shot. The jury acquitted him of the gun duel slaying, probably due to a lack of evidence.

But "Black Charley" couldn't stay out of trouble long.

In the summer of the following year, he was again indicted. This time for the murder of Mrs. Charles (Betty) Newton, 32, reputed to be his former girlfriend, and Jerry Meritt, 28. Their two bodies were found in a burned farmhouse less than a mile from Harris' trailer on Sunday, August 16, 1964. They had both been shot before the house was burned. Meritt had also testified against Charley in the 1963 murder trial.

Jerry Meritt's parents owned the farm. The two story frame house had been unoccupied since Mr. & Mrs. Courtney Meritt had moved into Fairfield more than a year before.

At first it was not known who the two charred bodies were but it was revealed the next morning that the two, a man and a woman, did not die accidental deaths. Officials revealed that x-rays of the two bodies showed more than one bullet hole in each head and these were being extracted by the pathologist and state crime lab men for tests.

It was suspected who the two might be because their families stated they had not returned home over the weekend.

State's Attorney Bill Pierce said the police were convinced the fire resulted from arson because a burning mattress found on top of the torsos had been doused with a chemical agent to make it burn intensely.

The fire was discovered about 8:15 a.m. by three hunters. Fire chief Richard Miller said, "We had just turned into the driveway and I smelled burning flesh and knew there were bodies in that fire . . ." The walls of the house were caved in and a car at the rear of the house was also aflame when the firemen arrived.

The next day Jerry Meritt's mother told the *Wayne County Press* that her son had spent the past year living in mortal fear for his life. She said, "He was scared to death . . . But just three weeks ago he told me, 'I can't run forever . . . if they're going to get me, it'll just have to happen.'"

It was thought that Meritt was in fear of Charley Harris because Meritt had testified against him in Harris' previous trial.

Asked if her son had ever received any threatening messages, she said she didn't think so, " . . . but he lived in constant fear. In fact he stayed home with us for nearly a year . . . hardly ever went up town . . . was even afraid to take a job." She also said he recently decided he couldn't go on living this way and planned to take a job, and also started going out more. He went to work for a local chemical company.

The paper asked her if her son had been keeping company with Betty Newton. Her response was, "She was scared to death, too. They were together all the time . . . he was the only one she had to look to."

Asked if Jerry mentioned anyone he feared she said, "Well, no. He was a boy who kept pretty much to himself."

She was also asked if she had any idea who might have killed her son. She responded, "You can't discuss that."

Mrs. Newton's elderly father, John Shockley, was also interviewed by the local paper. He said, "I hate to say it, but I am sure it's Betty." He said she wore dentures and a small wedding ring on one finger, and wore an Indian head ring on the other hand. The female victim's body wore dentures and a wedding ring was found on one hand, although the Indian head ring was not found. Mr. Shockley later became so overcome with grief, he was moved to the Memorial Hospital.

The car that was destroyed in the fire was a 1955 Plymouth, registered in the name of Betty's husband, Charles Newton. He had purchased it two month before the incident. The Newtons had five children and he had an older son by a previous marriage.

Mrs. Newton had told relatives she was going to go to St. Louis by bus that weekend to see her husband who was in a V-A hospital there, waiting to have surgery that Monday morning. After hearing that his wife may be dead, Mr. Newton left Sunday afternoon and returned home.

Even though it was known that Charley Harris had been "friendly" with Betty Newton, and Jerry Meritt had testified against Harris in his previous trial, State's Attorney Pearce denied reports from Evansville and St. Louis that local officers were looking for him. He emphasized that officers had no suspects at this time. He said Harris was at his Pond Creek home and was available if the police wanted him. He said, "He's never run away, has he?"

But there's always a first time for everything and this time, instead of bluffing it through, Charley Harris did run away. Charles Bryan "Black Charley" Harris took it on the lam and was now, not just on the run, he was on the FBI's list of "10 most wanted fugitives" in the United States. The FBI was seeking him for the Wayne County murders of Mrs. Betty Newton and Jerry Meritt when they caught him the following year, on June 17, 1965. He was found in his old neighborhood, in a deserted-looking farmhouse in the Pond Creek bottoms.

Harris was said to have told friends, "If the law wants me they'll have to shoot it out with me," but he was taken without resistance. Charles Woods, an FBI agent, said that one of the arresting party jumped between Harris and a loaded 22-caliber rifle he had near his reach.

The federal agents took him to Mount Carmel, where U.S. Commissioner George Woodcock turned him over to Wayne County Sheriff Gene Leathers. When they brought him back into the Wayne County jail, Charley said, "They caught me just as I was getting ready to shave. Now, maybe I can get a shave."

Chapter 21

Charley's Next Jail Term Doesn't End The Story

Charley Harris went on trial for the murders of Betty Newton and Jerry Meritt and, while the jury was out on November 3, 1965, the *Wayne County Press* came out with a special section, printed at 3 p.m. The four page spread showed all the photos covering the deadly fire scene and of those involved; the accused, the two victims and the prosecutor, appeared at the bottom of page one, and a two-page spread inside covered the deadly fire scene along with other details of the murders.

The editorial copy continued with the big local question, "Will the Charley Harris murder trial bring an end to a bloody era in old Pond Creek . . . an era that has seen it's name splashed in headlines the nation over as the continuing incidents of crime have been recorded there . . . or, will it bring the start of an entirely new reign of terror?

"The question was being kicked around by newsmen Wednesday as the jury deliberated the fate of Charlie Harris.

"'A good bet,' said one veteran reporter, 'is that the end of an era has come.' He reasoned it this way . . .

"Charley Harris is finished in Pond Creek, no matter what the jury does. If he goes to prison, it'll probably be a good long stretch and he's 69 already.

"If he goes free he'll never risk his neck going back down there where his property has been burned or destroyed, one piece after another.

"You don't have to travel far to find those who think that if the court fails to take care of Charley someone will.

"Some think he'll leave the country.

"Hence, in any event, they reason, Charley's Pond Creek days are ended."

"Now," some asked, "if Charley goes will the remaining Sheltons return?"

The answer to this was, "Big" Earl is the only member of the old gang living and he's 75 and the last his friends heard he was in Florida taking life easy. He's been very successful in real estate developments there, friends say."

Well, Black Charley Harris might have missed his shave when he was caught by the Feds but now, the only shave Charley would get would be to get his sentence "shaved" for good behavior for the two murders. He was convicted on November 3, 1965 and on December 10, was sentenced to 60 to 75 years in prison on each murder count, plus a term of 10 to 15 years for arson. The terms were to run concurrently. Charley declined to comment on the sentences but when he turned away from Circuit Judge Charles E. Jones his only comment was, "Thanks."

Charley's shave finally came in late 1980, when he was released from the Vienna, Illiinois center, after spending just 15 years in Illinois prisons.

And probably the most amazing fact about the life of "Black Charley" Harris is, how he died . . . and when.

Since his release from prison, Harris had made his home on the property owned by a niece, Bea Riley Kohler, in Elkhart, Kansas. He had visited Fairfield several times after his release, but he had his own small trailer on the Elkhart property and often ate his meals in the Kohler home.

On the evening of June 20, 1987, he had just seated himself at the supper table in the home, when he was stricken by a heart attack and fell to the floor. He was rushed to the Martin County Hospital, but it was too late.

"Black Charley" had died—*of natural causes . . . and at the age of 91!*

Graveside services were held in Elkhart on June 23, with his burial next to his wife, Rena Damon Harris, who had passed away in 1968. She was from New Harmony, Indiana. He was survived by a son, Weldon Harris, of Fairbury, Illinois and several nieces and nephews.

Now, you might think that this is finally the end of a fantastic story of the Sheltons and their friends and foes . . . but, again, it's not. **After all, some of the Sheltons were still alive!**

If the Shelton family lived in Indiana after they left Wayne County, it probably wasn't for long. They all later migrated to Florida, living mainly in the Jacksonville area, and on May 1, 1957, the matriarch of the family, Agnes Gaither Shelton, died there at the age of 91. Her obituary said she had been living in Jacksonville for about six years, which would have made it about 1951, the same year she left the Fairfield area.

Her survivors were listed as two sons, Earl and Dalta; two daughters, Mrs. Hazel McDonald and Lula Pennington, all of Jacksonville, Florida; and six grandchildren and seven great-grandchildren.

It wasn't until 1960 that the fourth Shelton brother would die, but this time it would be a non-violent cause. Dalta Shelton died of cancer in Jacksonville, Florida on December 22 of that year.

Dalta had been married twice; first to Mamie Conaway of Wayne County. They were divorced in 1912 and in 1914 he married Lillie Biggs. An infant child by his first wife, Mamie, had died and was buried in Wayne County. He had three children by his second wife, Lillie. They were Dorothy, born on June 21, 1916; Earl Benjamin (Little Earl) born on October 10, 1916 and Carl, (Little Carl) born in 1924.

As mentioned in Agnes Shelton's obituary, Lula Shelton Pennington had also moved to Jacksonville, Florida where she died on June 2, 1980. She was 71 years old and had since remarried. Lula had also been married before she married Guy Pennington.

She was first married to James Zuber and they were divorced. Then she married Guy. It was not stated if she outlived Guy Pennington or was divorced, but she later married Harry Barger. At her death, her name was listed as Lula Shelton Zuber Pennington Barger.

Moving from Fairfield was probably one of the wisest things "Big" Earl Shelton ever did, because he eventually died an old man, as opposed to being an early victim of an assassin's ambush.

Earl Robert Shelton (Big Earl) died on October 8, 1986, also in Jacksonville, Florida, at the ripe old age of 96. Funeral services were held at Hardage Giddens Guardian Chapel and burial was in Riverside Memorial Park there.

His obituary, sent to the *Wayne County Press* by his second wife, Earline McDaniel Shelton, said that he was retired from real estate developments in Florida and had been in declining health. He was also listed as a veteran of the U.S.Army in World War I. None of the stories carried a service record. The obit also states that he was survived by a sister, Hazel Zahn; nine nephews; and three nieces.

Hazel Shelton succeeded in outliving all of her brothers

and sisters. She must have either outlived Mr. McDonald or been divorced because her name is now listed on the family tree as Hazel Shelton McDonald Zahn and, at the time of this writing, was sill living, in St. Petersburg, Florida at the age of 93.

Also still alive were Dalta's two sons, "Little" Earl, and "Little" Carl.

Earl B. Shelton (Little Earl) still lived in Jacksonville, Florida and Carl Shelton (Little Carl) lived in Yulee, Florida, a suburb of Jacksonville.

The only other two remaining Sheltons (by marriage) then were Pearl, Carl's widow, and Genevieve, Bernie's widow.

Chapter 22

What Happened To Pearl Shelton?

Opal Pearl Vaughan Shelton was still living in Peoria in 1950, while the Sheltons were being used for target practice in Fairfield. After inheriting half of Carl Shelton's estate, she still had business to take care of. One of the most important items was to liquidate some of Carl's holdings, mainly the land he had owned in Wayne County.

The rest of the family, who were also heirs of Carl's, were not of a mind to sell any of his land at this point. But the only way she could get her share was to liquidate Carl's holdings by filing a partition suit. To do this, her attorney advised her to deed all of her land holdings over to a bank, in trust. That way the bank could represent her in its name alone. She and her attorney contacted the Commercial National Bank of Peoria, and Sylvan Olson, the bank's trust officer, agreed to handle the matter for her.

The Commercial Bank took the case to the Circuit Court of Wayne County to force liquidation of the holdings. The suit named the Commercial Bank (as the plaintiff) vs. Earl R. Shelton, Dalta Shelton, Agnes Shelton, Lulu (Lula) Shelton Pennington, Hazel Shelton McDonald, Wesley A. Shelton, Willard A. Shelton,

Blanche Shelton in her personal right, Blanche Shelton as administrator of the estate of Roy Shelton, deceased, and Genevieve Shelton, as defendants.

A notice was posted on March 14, 1951 of a "Master's Land Sale" to be held at 1:00 p.m. on the 7th day of April, 1951. The partition suit's public auction took place at the south door of the Wayne County court house in Fairfield. Seven parcels of land were auctioned off, excluding the mineral rights, while one parcel was sold, including the mineral rights.

After this forced auction, Pearl was no longer in good favor with the family and she was almost certainly not popular with the enemies of the Sheltons. It wasn't a comfortable situation for her.

It was on August 15, 1951, she gave her lawyer power of attorney in her affairs and headed for California to live with an aunt in Oakland, California. In September 1951, Pearl was settled in with her aunt at 365 Hanover Avenue in Oakland. She rented an adjoining apartment.

She was still dating the man she had been seeing before Carl died, and wrote back to friends in Peoria that she was concerned about "Lover Boy," who had apparently gone with her to Oakland. He had left there to return home and told her he would call her from Chicago the next day, but he hadn't called. In the letter she also said, "This pretending that I'm happy and everything is fine is a lot of hooey. Altho I'm trying very hard, and will *manage* to stick it out, for I do know there's nothing else to do. But believe me it isn't easy."

On January 24 of the next year, Pearl wrote back to Peoria friends again, indicating that all was well under control so far but she hoped she would be fortunate enough to keep things that way. She said in this letter that she had been back in Chicago to visit "Lover Boy" but wondered how he and "Uncle Sam" were getting along. Since he was not in service, it's believed that she may have been referring to his situation with Uncle Sam's Internal Revenue Service.

In another letter dated April 1, 1953 Pearl said she had since moved from the aunt's location in Oakland to 2208 Lakeshore Avenue, Apt. 206 in the same city.

She was now talking about another man named "John," she was apparently going with. She told of taking a trip with him to Los Angeles, where they stayed at the swank Ambassador Hotel, but pointed out they were in adjoining rooms.

Then, on July 14, 1954, she wrote again, but this time her stationery read "Mrs. John E. Upphoff, 140 Lexford Road, Piedmont, California." In this letter she indicated she and her new husband, John, had visited Peoria recently and were thanking friends for their hospitality.

She and John Emil Upphoff, an executive of the F.W. Woolworth Company in Oakland, California, were married on Saturday June 6, 1954, at the Piedmont Community Church in Piedmont, California.

After this, Peoria friends heard less and less of Pearl. One reason may have been that her new husband wanted her to sever old ties. But the Uphoffs seemed to continue a happy life in California for quite some time.

Sometime after this, John and Pearl Uphoff moved back to Fairfield, Illinois. Why? It's hard to speculate, except to reason that the old gang wars between the families of Shelton, Harris and Vaughan (she was a Vaughan) had now been over for many years and, as Pearl got older, she wanted to be near her family again.

And, ironically, Bernie's widow, Genevieve Shelton, did the same thing about Bernie's holdings after his death that Pearl Shelton had done. She walked off with a major part of his fortune but, unknown to Bernie, she already had a personal attorney.

She had hired him while Bernie was still alive, because she had money of her own she didn't want Bernie to know about, so she had her attorney handle it for her. The same attorney later handled her interests with regard to Bernie's holdings.

The moral to this story is: When it comes to money, illegal or not, gangsters families just can't trust anybody, not even their wives!

Chapter 23

"Who Done It" To Carl And Bermie Shelton?

But now, with all the other major players of the Shelton gang gone, with the possible exception of "Little" Earl, it now seems the appropriate time to drop the curtain on one of the most fascinating and complicated stories of gangs and gangsters in Illinois' colorful history.

And it's hard to drop that curtain without having found who actually did kill Carl and Bernie Shelton.

If you believe that Carl knew he was talking to "Black Charley" Harris just before he died, that might be correct. But even if Charley fingered Carl, or was the killer himself, he had to have outside help from some unknown gang . . . and the fact that it was even Charley ***has never been proven in court!***

As for the murderer of Bernie Shelton, it's been speculated that a St. Louis or Chicago gang, or even a syndicate between the two, were the one's responsible. But, again, who pulled the trigger?

Another possibility was that it was Pete Petrakos who had mysteriously disappeared at the time of Bernie's killing and just as mysteriously reappeared the night after Bernie was killed. Was Pete Bernie's killer?

Or could it have been Roy Gatewood? He certainly

had the motive, based on the records Bernie and Jack Ashby made of him being the middleman between Bernie and the State's Attorney.

Or could it have been Roy P. Hull, the State's Attorney himself? Bernie had really put him on the spot regarding a suspected shakedown for $25,000.

Or, finally, could it have been Clyde Garrison? There had been a lot of bad blood between the two, ever since the Shelton gang came to town and knocked him out of his "kingpin" spot as head of the Peoria gamblers.

Well, there's one man who believes he knows how Bernie was killed and where the killer came from and just how it happened. It's John Lucas, the grand-nephew of Clyde Garrison.

In his recent statement, John said that Clyde's sister, Nell, who was also John's grandmother, told him the story, personally, a couple of years before she died.

She told her grandson that ***she was in Clyde's apartment in the Jefferson Hotel when Clyde was talking by phone to people in Chicago about coming down and killing Bernie Shelton!***

John said the family story is that someone in the rackets in Chicago sent a man down to Peoria to do the job.

According to this story, the man came in on the Rock Island Rocket train, probably the day before. He borrowed Garrison's girlfriend's green Chevrolet and drove it (or had someone else drive it) to West Peoria, to somewhere above the Parkway Tavern, where the car was parked. Then the killer walked halfway down the bluff behind the tavern and shot Bernie when he came out to his car from the tavern that morning. Then he laid the rifle down (without fingerprints), walked up the bluff to the getaway car and drove away.

Lucas said that he doubts that this was the same green Chevrolet that followed the ambulance that Bernie saw.

What probably got Bernie's attention was that he knew that Clyde Garrison's girlfriend had a green Chevrolet and that's why he yelled to the ambulance attendant to watch the car that was following them.

Finally, according to the Garrison family story, the killer went back to Chicago, probably that same afternoon, on the Rock Island Rocket!

But, again, no one saw the killer, except possibly Garrison and his girlfriend, and no one seems to have known exactly who he was. Also, no one has ever been charged with the murder.

So at this late date, we may know *how* Bernie was eliminated, but the odds are we'll never know **who actually pulled the trigger that killed Bernie Shelton!**

Post Script

It was near the end of writing this book I found out that Pearl Shelton Uphoff had moved back to Fairfield, Illinois. I called the publisher of the Wayne County Press, identified myself and told him I was writing a book about the Sheltons. I asked him if he could help me locate a lady named Pearl Uphoff. He said he could but, before he did, he asked me to explain why I wanted to talk to her regarding the Sheltons. I said, "because Pearl Uphoff is Carl Shelton's widow."

The man was nearly speechless. He indicated that he had known her for years and had been a neighbor of hers at one time but he ***NEVER KNEW SHE WAS CARL SHELTON'S WIDOW!***

Well, I suppose that's understandable. Pearl certainly didn't need the publicity and it probably rarely, if ever, came up in neighborly conversation!

I eventually did get Pearl's address and phone number. If she was 35 when she married Carl Shelton in 1947, she would be 85 now.

I called the number and a younger female voice answered the phone. I said I was from Peoria and asked to talk to Mrs. Uphoff. The young woman asked me to wait while she apparently went into another room. I could barely hear a conversation.

When Pearl was told I was calling from Peoria, she answered the phone. Her voice was very weak and she advised me that I'd have to talk loud because she was hard of hearing. She also indicated that she was quite ill.

I told her that I was writing a story on the Shelton family and would like to talk to her. She immediately said, "No, I won't discuss it. That's all in the past and that's where it's going to stay."

I tried to say more but she wouldn't answer, so I thanked her for speaking with me and told her that, if she changed her mind, to get in touch, repeating my name and number.

I understood Pearl's reluctance to discuss painful times of the past, but I didn't necessarily want to talk about the Sheltons and the gang.

Reading this story would indicate that there was no lack of information on the gangs and clans. What I really wanted to know more about was her life after this colorful era. More about her second husband and their life together, in what must have been almost tranquility compared to the roaring days of the past.

Shortly after that phone conversation with Pearl Vaughan Shelton Uphoff, she passed away.

I remember those days of the Sheltons in Peoria. I never met any of them, although I had seen Carl and others on the street. I will confess I played some of their slot machines and punch boards, and I knew it wasn't healthy in our town to be at odds with any of them.

But one of the things that stands out in my mind is, how little danger there was to the average every day person living in Peoria in those times. We all went about our business somewhat oblivious to what was going on around us.

So, I'll just leave you with one anecdote about Carl Shelton.

Just before I resigned as manager of the Madison Theater in the late 1950's, I heard a story from my boss, Len Worley, the city manager of our Great States Theaters.

He told about the time he was relieving Merle Eagle as manager of the Palace Theater while Merle took a vacation.

The fire department had been cracking down on safety in all the downtown public gathering places. The Palace had a fire escape in the alley, just across from "The Pub," a saloon in that alley. The last section of the fire escape had a counter-weight that kept it up in the air until it lowered with the weight of people coming down the steps.

But the area directly under the fire escape was a convenient place to park a car and it was often used for that unlawful purpose.

So the fire marshall told management in no uncertain terms that they had the responsibility of keeping the area clear.

On a busy Saturday night Len went around to check the area and found a man sitting there in his car. Worley politely told the man he'd have to move and why. A few minutes later Len went back out to look, and the guy was still sitting there.

Worley had a short fuse when riled, and he was riled. He proceeded to tell this "punk" who he was and what he was going to do, if he didn't move his car . . . and NOW!

Len said this fellow just sat there listening to his tirade as though he really didn't care much, one way or the other. When Len had finished "telling him off," the man said, "Now I know who you are, but do you know who I am?" Len gruffly told him no, and he really didn't care. At this point the man quietly replied, "I'm Carl Shelton."

After Len's heart beat returned to something near normal, all he could answer was a very meek "Yes sir."

When Len told me this story years later, I jokingly asked, "Well, Len, didn't you have him arrested or anything?" Len replied, "Hell, no! That's pretty obvious, isn't it?" "What's so obvious?" I retorted. Len shot back, "I'm still here to tell about it, ain't I?"

He was right, of course, it was pretty obvious . . . ***and it seems like only yesterday!***

Bibliography

Peoria Journal
Peoria Star
Peoria Journal Star
Peoria News
West Bluff Word (Peoria) Oct. 1986)
Chicago Daily News
Chicago Herald-American
Chicago Tribune
St. Louis Post-Dispatch
Ted Link, reporter, St. Louis Post-Dispatch
Dickson Terry, reporter, St. Louis Post-Dispatch
St. Louis Globe Democrat
Wayne County Press (Files of)
"A Knight of Another Sort" by Gary DeNeal
"Charlie Birger, Southern Illinois' Very Own Gangster" by Gary DeNeal (Outdoor Illinois magazine)
"Barbarians in Our Midst" Peterson—1952
"Gang Wars in Southern Illinois" by Linda Pierce (Illinois History magazine)
Illinois History magazine—Dec. 1974
"Little Egypt" Bedlinger's—1973
"The Sheltons: America's Bloodiest Gang" by John Bartlow Martin (Saturday Evening Post—March 18, 1950)
"The Shelton Boys" by John Bartlow Martin (from the book, "The Butcher's Dozen)

"Terror in Southern Illinois" by Harry B. Wilson (Esquire magazine)

"The Vice That Was Peoria" by former mayor of Peoria, Carl O. Triebel. (Saturday Evening Post)

"Wyatt Earp's Lost Year" by Roger Jay (Wild West magazine August 2003)

Testimony before the Peoria County Grand Jury, called by Peoria County State's Attorney, Roy P. Hull, asking for an investigation of alleged attempted bribery charges. Testimony from Aug. 23, 1948 through Sept. 2, 1948.

A phone conversation with Tom Matthews, Jr., Publisher of the Wayne County Press.

A phone conversation with Mrs. Pearl Uphoff, (Carl Shelton's widow.)

A conversation with John Lucas, grand-nephew of Clyde Garrison.

A conversation with Jack Heintzman.

A conversation with Tony Couri

A conversation with Ed LaHood

Printed in the United States
203251BV00002B/17/A

9 781413 460124